Tom Chetwynd was born in London in 1938, educated at Downside School and studied Theology at London University. His mother, Bridget Chetwynd, was a novelist, and he himself started writing at the age of seventeen, with an impulse to record a vivid waking dream that appeared in his first novel, *Rushing Nowhere*. After an intensive period of exploring his own unconscious — which resulted in novels, scripts and stories written in symbolic language — he turned his attention to dreams and produced his *Dictionary for Dreamers* which has enabled many people to discover the value and significance of their own dreams. Since the success of this dictionary, he has been able to concentrate on the wider significance of symbolism as a whole, not only as it affects the individual through his own personal waking dreams, but also as it appeals to his unconscious through myths, fairy-tales, religion, literature, art and cinema. The last years have seen a major breakthrough in the understanding of the value and meaning of symbolism — that there is only one symbolic language which is used by dreams, creative imagination and myths in expressing the unconscious, the imagination and the soul — and his subsequent *Dictionary of Symbols* and *Dictionary of Sacred Myth* have been compiled largely from the fruits of this recent research.

LANGUAGE OF THE UNCONSCIOUS
VOLUME 1

Dictionary for Dreamers

TOM CHETWYND

Thorsons
An Imprint of HarperCollins*Publishers*

Thorsons
An Imprint of HarperCollins*Publishers*
77–85 Fulham Palace Road,
Hammersmith, London W6 8JB

Published by George Allen & Unwin Ltd 1972
Published by Paladin Books 1974
Aquarian Press edition 1993
10 9 8 7

A catalogue record for this book
is available from the British Library

ISBN 1 85538 295 4

Printed and bound in Great Britain by
Caledonian International Book Manufacturing Ltd, Glasgow

Acknowledgements

This dictionary is a selection of the most significant discoveries of the last seventy years about the mysterious nature, the hidden meanings, and the purpose of dreams, arranged in a manner intended to help the individual to understand his own dreams. It is particularly indebted to the works of Sigmund Freud, Carl G. Jung, Wilhelm Stekel, also Calvin S. Hall, Ernest Jones, J. Layard, Gerhard Adler, Jolande Jacobi, Edward C. Whitmont, and Emil A. Gutheil, as well as to others listed in the bibliography (pp. 193-4).

For complete alphabetical index of all subjects covered in this Dictionary, see page 195.

Dreams as Part of the
Creative Process

Dreams are part of the process of human evolution, and whether the individual notices it or not, dreams will always be contributing to his efforts to fulfil the whole of his potential, concentrating especially on those parts that he is neglecting and that are therefore threatening the growth and development of his personality.

If it is true that men have evolved from something resembling sponges – if the most primitive matter has gradually been refined over the ages, first into the sense of touch, then into the eye that sees, and finally into that most complex and sensitive of living organisms, the human mind with its intellect, memory and imagination – then there is plainly a spontaneous process of growth at work in nature that does not depend on anybody's being aware of it. Nevertheless, there is all the difference between continually thwarting and frustrating its activities – at the expense of a lot of fruitless energy – and becoming increasingly aware of our own inner needs and cooperating with them.

Dreams tell us what we need, as well as what we desire, in order to be complete. Dreaming involves directing the dreamer's attention especially to whatever he is most in danger of ignoring or rejecting in his everyday waking attitudes.

Often when the individual's outlook is becoming too rigid or limited, dreams give the other side of the picture. Jung realized that Freud found so much sexual content in dreams because he, like so many other people at that time, denigrated sexuality. Similarly, if people exclude all altruism and wonder from their waking thoughts, their dreams would call attention to this.

Jung also made a clear distinction between the idea of being 'perfect' and being 'whole': that is, developing every aspect of the personality, every faculty of the mind, and using all the senses, including sexuality, to their utmost – but never one at the expense of another. Even the most spiritual and intellectual attitudes may threaten this wholeness if they are too exclusive and don't give due regard to the emotions and the flesh. And this seems to be the underlying purpose of dreams: to restore the balance between the various parts of the personality so that they complement rather than destroy each other.

This cannot be achieved without inner conflict, and dreams often express this underlying tension, which, although it may be accompanied by yearning and suffering, seems to stir mankind to its greatest efforts and so often accompanies all true growth, progress or discovery.

Dreams have been described as the 'dress rehearsal' for life. As this implies, they cover much varied ground, trying out many possibilities that the future could hold in store, before the flesh-and-blood live performance is acted out once and for all. Their scope (in the realm of the potential) is enormous: they are far too free and extravagant to be fitted into any kind of mould, but they do all arise from the most primitive part of the mind and are determined more by the strength of the emotions within than by any other consideration. It is this primitive and emotional content that is their essential value. Through them the individual can make contact with the roots of his being and his own true needs. When his integrity is destroyed, his inner security weakened or his power to love impoverished, for example, he can still remain face to face with the creative sources within that reveal the meaning and the value of his existence, in contrast with his superficial aims, pressures or influences that are not in accord with his nature. In a crisis, when his life is particularly threatened by outside circumstances or inner stultification, a person usually has his most vivid and meaningful dreams, and these will be all the more effective if he pays attention to them and respects them.

Dreams are also disconcertingly honest, so that unless the individual is prepared to be completely sincere, it is a waste of time to unearth their hidden meaning, only to reject it out of hand.

The Most Important Principles of Dream Interpretation

Noting the Dream

People who have difficulty recalling their dreams should try not to wake up too abruptly, but should lie in a passive and relaxed state for a moment or two. Sometimes an effort to remember the first thought that came into their heads on waking may not only bring back the dream but may also be relevant to its hidden meaning.

Alternatively, later in the day some incident may remind the individual of his dream, and in the same way the relationship between the incident and the dream may throw light on the dream itself.

The dream – noted accurately and without any omissions, however embarrassing, and without any additions or changes, however much they help to make it superficially more coherent – always remains the vital, central and inviolate factor in the art of interpretation. The more clearly it is impressed on the mind, by being written out, or by any part of it being drawn or painted that seems to invite that (regardless of skill), the more effective it will be.

The interpretation is never a substitute for the dream itself, but only adds to the vividness and vitality of the images. Worst of all would be to impose some arbitrary interpretation; far better to dwell on the dream itself in all its obscurity than to try to fit it into some unconvincing mould of the rational mind.

The Ideas and Memories that Arise Spontaneously Around Each Image in the Dream

Only the dreamer himself can be sure, finally, whether his dream has been interpreted correctly or not. All that somebody else – even the most experienced analyst – can do is to help elicit the meaning of a dream from the dreamer's own unconscious. And as every analyst knows, his participation complicates this process because it necessarily brings into play the personality and prejudices of the analyst himself, along with those of the dreamer. Fortunately, where there is no mental block, no refusal to accept oneself as one is, all that an individual needs to interpret his own dreams successfully is sufficient information about the way dreams work. And that is what this dictionary is designed to supply.

Perhaps the most important principle to bear in mind is that the person who fabricated the dream did so with a part of his own mind, and although once he is awake he doesn't have any access to it, nevertheless at the back of his mind he already knows what his dream means. Many concrete examples of the way dream images often work will be valuable only if they are used to jog the mind, like so much else that is stored in our minds but that we can't recall until something, however trivial, brings it to the surface.

Under hypnosis people can apparently interpret their dreams without any difficulty – although afterwards they may refuse to believe that the images have any meaning at all. This is why the dreamer can be fairly confident of recognizing the correct interpretation of his dream when he sees it – as long as he isn't in the habit of deceiving himself.

Many of the images in dreams could never be found in any dictionary of dreams, however comprehensive, because they are formed from personal experience and are thus unique. In order to discover the meaning of such images, it is important to note anything that comes to mind in association with the incidents, people, background, etc., in the dream. This seems to be done best by relaxing into a state as near as possible to the dream state, releasing all conscious control over one's thoughts – until they wander too far from the point. At first it is important to be open to the greatest possible range of meanings that may come to mind spontaneously. Sleep releases the mind from the ordinary strictures of society and the inner restrictions of conscience; it is this detached state in which, by using his intuition and emotions rather than logic and will, the individual is most likely to unravel them.

Only after that is it worth concentrating on the images and

trying to discern their meanings, with particular reference to which aspect of the individual's life they may be related – whether the sexual sphere, the outside world or the inner realm. An individual's dreams are nearly always concerned with his personal problems, and only he knows these well enough to recognize the links between the dream and his present situation and any relevant past experience.

Then it may be worth trying to identify with each of the images in the dream in turn, pretending to be the bird, the dream-figure, the swimming pool, etc. Since the dream is a fabrication, an extension of one's own mind, this method of letting the mind become each of the images can be revealing.

It is important to bear in mind that dreams occur mostly in the form of images. They use a pictorial language that may not be very precise but compensates by being astonishingly vivid. It is, in fact, the oldest language in the world, the only universal language the human race has ever developed, and the one in which an image of a tree represents not only the tree but everything associated with it in the human mind.

Especially if a dream is long and complicated, it may help to pick out the significant factors and get the overall impression. It is also helpful to search for its possible purpose, which Jung considered the most important element in interpretation.

A Series of Dreams

Because one dream often throws light on another, far more satisfactory results can be obtained from trying to interpret them in groups, rather than looking at each dream in isolation.

There seems to be sufficient evidence that once the individual starts trying to understand his dreams, the dream-mind co-operates, using images that the dreamer has come to understand, and if he fails to understand the message, restating it in clearer and more vivid images in later dreams. This does not mean that an individual can dictate the actual contents of a dream, however; only that it may appear in a more explicit form.

It is over a lifetime that the pattern of dreams, and its true bearing on the individual's life, emerges most clearly.

Not Just Dreams

Understanding the symbolism and imagery of dreams throws light on poetry, painting, religious ritual, myth, fairy tale and any activity that arises spontaneously and autonomously from the depths of the mind. It is possible, especially for an artist, to make contact with these regions of the mind while still awake and become aware of the particular contents of his own unconscious. Such material can be interpreted like dreams.

How to Interpret your own Dreams

How To Use the Dictionary

Although the individual should gradually become increasingly familiar with the way dreams work simply by using the dictionary it is nevertheless advisable to have some idea of the principles behind modern interpretation (p. 9) and a basic understanding of such categories in the dictionary as ARCHETYPES, CONFLICT, EMOTIONS, MIND, WORD PLAY, etc.

For the sake of convenience, to save repetition and because of the way images are often related to and complement one another, the index (page 195), with every image listed in alphabetical order, will be helpful until the reader gets used to the way the various images are grouped and arranged in the book. Where several entries are grouped under a main heading – for example, BUILDINGS or ANIMALS – it is usually advisable to read the introductory paragraph for the general significance, since any particular significance will be mentioned only where it adds to or contradicts this general significance.

By gradually absorbing the way the dream-mind forms its images, by observing such links as there are between the image and what it represents, by noticing the kind of resemblance and the sort of association employed, the individual should soon begin to recognize the implications of even the most personal and unique of images.

At first it is worth noting whether an image resembles, in shape or in function, what it signifies. Or a link may exist because the word for the object in the dream has another, completely different meaning. Alternatively, a similarity in number, in colour or in value to the dreamer could be sufficient connection.

Anything in the world may be used to express the feelings and thoughts coming from the depths of the mind – but the individual who formed the image can usually discover how to reverse the process. This is often a question of picking. out the main characteristics of the image – for example, a penguin is a bird (§),* is inedible and can't fly – and then seeing in what way this could be applied to the dreamer's life.

Many of the images have more than one interpretation because while they mean one thing to one person in particular circumstances, they mean something quite different to somebody else in another situation. Discovering which meaning is applicable should be a question of recognition, a feeling that this is near the mark. Where there is no such feeling, it can only be hoped that the listed alternatives will spark off another, completely fresh possibility in the dreamer's mind. (And growing familiarity with the dictionary should enable an individual to gain fresh insights from other listed images that may, superficially, have very little connection with a particular dream whose meaning is being sought.)

Never before have so many images and symbols been collected in one book, all taken from genuine dreams to which a satisfying and valid interpretation was found. It is when these many isolated insights are juxtaposed that the patterns of dream-thought (the way dreams work in practice) begin to emerge more clearly than ever before.

The fact remains that the images in dreams are as many and varied as the universe itself, and no dictionary, however comprehensive, could list them all with their many permutations and combinations. However, it is equally true that when a dreamer studies his overall dream pattern, the particular intricacies of each dream begin to fall into place.

Sometimes it is no more than one clue that spans the gulf between everyday thought processes and those of a dream; by means of this clue we can cross the bridge into the unconscious with a new understanding of its contents, which is the aim of interpretation. At other times the whole dream may be 'typical' and an interpretation that has been meaningful many times in the past is totally applicable. But even so, it is still risky to substitute the explanation for the dream. By doing so, the individual remains stuck in the same arid and limited area of rational concepts as before, instead of entering a new realm with its own vivid pictorial language.

* See pages 17-18 for explanation of symbols.

Of course the images in a particular dream may have direct and obvious associations for the dreamer which must be explored first, and cannot be ignored even though the dream may also have a symbolic significance as Freud thought. This dictionary refers only to the symbolic meanings.

Dream interpretation cannot be equated with psychoanalysis, and although this book draws largely on the discoveries and insights of psychoanalysts – the result of much painstaking and empirical research – the fruit of their work can be seen to have a far wider application. Whereas dream interpretation forms only a small part of the analyst's work, so psychoanalysis is only one application of interpreting dreams. Just as the analysts necessarily drew the material for their work from every source – myth, religion, art, alchemy, etc. – so their work bears fruit in the general sphere of life itself.

This book is intended for the mass of intelligent people who do not consult an analyst but are nevertheless interested in their own dreams (whether for the sheer delight of it – not unlike the delight of seeing a newspaper astrological forecast that happens to fit the day's events – or in a more serious quest of self-knowledge). It is not meant for the emotionally troubled or seriously upset. Prevention is better than cure!

As this dictionary covers the whole range of research since the turn of the century, there are many instances in which past attitudes could not be omitted without the simultaneous loss of a genuine and valuable insight. And it would have been impossible to eliminate entirely the prevailing attitude towards women on the part of the men who were working in this field often more than fifty years ago.

Abbreviations Used in the Dictionary

Asterisks mean: Points to, signifies, indicates, depicts, or refers to. (This may be the result of tradition, association with myth, or word-play, etc.)

***: *Usually* points to, indicates.
 **: *May* point to, indicate.
  *: *Could* point to, indicate.

Where asterisks open a new paragraph, what follows is an

alternative interpretation of the main heading in bold type at the top of that particular entry.

(§) or (§ FOLLOWED BY WORD OR PHRASE): See, See also, Compare; and indicates textual cross-references.

BOLDFACE CAPITALS indicate the specific dream images.

Boldface type indicates specific examples within broad categories (for example, **Cat** in the section on **ANIMALS**).

Italic type indicates variations on or examples of dream images.

†: Conflict. The possible underlying conflict.

/: The contrast between what is on either side of the slash.

v.: Versus, for giving the two sides of a conflict.

Quotation marks: Indicate plays on words or metaphoric usages (except where they simply denote a quotation).

ABANDONMENT A necessary preliminary to being independent; may occur in the dreams of young people about to go out on their own.

ACCIDENT (Misfortune)
Happening to the dreamer: ** He is punishing himself, in a token way, to appease his conscience (§ PUNISHMENT). ** The lengths to which the unconscious (§ MIND) is at present prepared to go in order to avoid responsibilities, difficulties or decisions; it may later find a more effective means.
Happening to somebody else in the dream: ** Aggression towards that person, though the dreamer has superficially avoided responsibility.

The ACTION of the Dream Nothing appears in the dream that the dreamer didn't put there. *However much the 'I' of the dream is sorry, tries to rescue the other figures, or alter the action,* he nevertheless remains responsible for everything else that takes place as well. (§ ACCIDENT, ATTITUDE, DEATH.)

AGGRESSION ** Aggressive impulses that have been stifled in waking life but are still breeding resentment in the depths of the unconscious.

If given no other outlet these aggressive impulses may turn against the individual himself; become self-destructive. However this same impulse can be transformed into sacrifice (§), so long as that sacrifice is consciously reckoned with, and deliberately undertaken. (§ RELIGIOUS IMAGERY, Christ suffering.)

Somebody else may seem to be the aggressor, while the dreamer appears to be the victim or innocent bystander, isolated from the violence or even appalled by it. Yet the dream may still be revealing something about the dreamer's underlying aggression, how he proposes to handle these impulses and the possible consequences. As long as the conscious mind recognizes this basic impulse of survival, it can usually come to terms with it.

Aggression suffered by the dreamer: ** Some aspect of the dreamer's life is being menaced by the aggressor, who, once he is identified (§ PEOPLE), may turn out to be the last person the dreamer would have recognized as a threat in waking life.

Aggressor, victim, enclosure: * The parents, formerly protective and helpful, have now become destructive to the growth of the individual. This theme recurs in the dreams of young people due to leave home and the family circle, the enclosure.

** Sexual passion. Aggression and passion are often not differentiated in dreams. *Thus, being hit with a stick or otherwise assaulted, especially in women's dreams:* ** Sexual assault. *Being assaulted by someone of the same sex:* ** Passive homosexuality.

Being exaggeratedly aggressive and violent, in a man's dreams: ** Determination to conceal the feminine side of his nature even from himself (§ ARCHETYPES, Anima).

ANIMALS *** The animal vitality in the dreamer: either the body with its instinctive sexual cravings, or the sub-human and 'bestial' impulses of the unconscious.

Trying to find some refuge from animals, whether by building fences or shoring up inadequate buildings, etc.: ** The dreamer's struggle with his animal instincts. The dream may indicate whether the precautions being taken are adequate or if more is required. These instincts may be threatening or damaging other aspects of the individual's life.

Taming or harnessing the animals: ** The dreamer's efforts to control his instincts and if possible render them constructive, useful.

Killing the animal: Managing to restrain the animal is better than killing it, which may at the same time destroy the vital energy derived from the instincts.

Eating the animal: ** Reassimilating the energy.

** Other people, especially the parents. *If the sex of the animals is not indicated, then the larger may represent the father and the smaller the mother:* The dream could be about repressed wishes and fears centring on infantile sexuality, which is often incestuous.

** Aspects of the unconscious that are superior in certain respects to ordinary human attitudes.

Talking animals, wise, awe-inspiring, or godlike animals: Animals are superior to man because they have not yet blundered into consciousness or pitted their self-will against the power from which they derive life. It is always important to pay attention to this aspect of animal life in fairy tales and dreams (Jung). ** The Self (§ ARCHETYPES).

Helpful animals: ** Helpful stirrings of the unconscious, probably rendered cooperative because the conscious attitude is positive and 'right'.

Baby animals ** Children (especially, 'kid', 'lamb', etc.).
Animals that never grow up (the runt pig, etc.): ** Infantilism. The dreamer's inability to mature or to face life.
Animal with a cub: ** Motherliness, and therefore the mother.

Bear ** The Mother (§ FAMILY); the Great Mother (§ ARCHETYPES); 'bearing' children, and caring for them.
Hugging to death: ** The possessive devouring mother. * An 'overbearing' person, a 'bear' of a man; possibly the father. * To 'bare', to expose.

Bull *** Sexual passion, as creative power or, more often in its negative aspect, blind rage, destructive brute compulsions.
Slaying the bull: ** Initiation into the world of the mature adult, who masters his instincts in order not to be at their mercy. (§ WILD ANIMALS, Dangerous Animals.)

Cat ** The feline, the catlike in human beings, usually in women; the elegant but also the uncanny of witches' familiars and Egyptian gods. (§ SINISTER ANIMALS.)

Chameleon * Adaptability.

Cold-blooded animals ** The cold, unrelated, inhuman aspect of the instincts.

Composite animals ** The various qualities of the different animals of which they are made up. Two potentials of development in one figure.
Half animal, half man: ** the animal instincts are beginning to be humanized.

Cow ** Providing milk, nourishment. The eternal feminine, especially the mother (§ FAMILY) or mother figure (§ ARCHETYPES).

Deformed animals ** The dreamer thinks of his impulses as repugnant, revolting.

Dog ** The 'dogged' or doglike in people. The faithful and devoted companion, or somebody the dreamer can't shake off and who might make trouble (depending on the rest of the dream but also on the dreamer's waking attitude to dogs).
A dog belonging to someone: * That person.
A dog that the dreamer owned or knew at some period of his life: * That period of his life.
A huntress with dogs: ** The Amazon/Huntress Self or Anima (§ ARCHETYPES).
A dog guarding some gates, near a cemetery, etc.: The fact that dogs devour corpses may account for their being the guardians of the underworld (Cerberus); 'the hounds of Hell'; creatures that must be pacified and put to sleep before the dreamer can pass through the underworld (§ EARTH, Underworld).

Domesticated animals (Tame animals) Passions under control; also suggests that those passions were never very formidable.

Elephant * Earth (§). The Self (§ ARCHETYPES), radiant and glowing.

Frog Transforms from a tadpole and moves on to the land.
* A period of transformation (frog into prince?). (§ SNAKE, as all reptiles have the same significance.)

Goat ** Lasciviousness, procreation (Pan, Satan). Those who will be sorted from the sheep. The dark side of human nature.
Riding a goat: ** The dreamer's relationship with the dark side of his nature.

Hare Swift, curious, fearful and leaps. ** Intuition, spiritual insight; intuitive 'leaps'. In its warped, negative aspect intuition may be degraded by fear or ignorance into madness: 'mad as a March hare'.
** The Priestess/Witch or the Trickster/Black Magician (§ ARCHETYPES; §SACRIFICE, for killing, cooking, or sacrificing the hare).
Radiant hare, holding its baby in a cave: * The Mother of God.

Horns ** The orgiastic experience of natural instinctive life. Horns belong to Pan and the Devil. But also (if the animals or demigod horned creatures are radiant) the positive aspect of phallic power, which is fertility and creation. Or the positive and negative aspects of a conflict. Or problem: 'the horns of a dilemma'. Or adultery: making the cuckold 'wear horns'.

Horse ** The energy at a man's disposal.
The horse under strain or dying: ** A severe weakening of this dynamic power that carries a man forward ('horsepower'); it is important to note the forces or circumstances that are weakening or killing it.
A winged horse: * The poetic imagination; being harnessed to a cart indicates that it is being abused for thoroughly utilitarian purposes.
** A ruling passion, an instinct that carries the dreamer away.
In a man's dream: ** A woman; or the Anima, the realm of the feminine (§ ARCHETYPES).
In a woman's dream, being kicked – especially in the stomach by

the hind leg of the horse – or otherwise attacked: ** The desire to be taken sexually by an ardent lover.

A black horse: * The unruliness of the passions (§ COLOURS).

Someone on a pale horse: * Death.

A horse that can get through any door and batter down all obstacles: ** The collective Shadow (§ ARCHETYPES).

The horse as beast of burden: ** The Mother, or Mother Archetype (§; § RIDING). In modern dreams the car (§ JOURNEYS) has largely taken over from the horse as a symbol with many of the same associations.

* Unconscious energy, which the individual may be preparing to use in his service by giving it the necessary attention.

Lion ** 'Devouring' appetite, 'raging' desire, brute force, unredeemed instinct.

The struggle with the lion: This should mark a successful stage in maturing as long as the dreamer is not overpowered, or the lion killed.

A man-eating lion can roam free in the jungle but not in the villages: The image of the dream is much clearer and more vivid than any explanation about how everything has its proper place.

A lion lying with a lamb: ** A union, or compatability of opposites; instinct and spirit going hand in hand.

** Pride or courage.

Lizard * One-track thinking.

Monkey ** The infantile, childish and arrested side of the dreamer's character; in the womb the foetus goes through a re-enactment of the phases of evolution, and at one stage has something in common with the monkey, which always sits in the embryo position. No wonder it has become the image of regressive tendencies, whether towards the primitive and sub-human or the specifically childish. * Ape of God, and therefore the Devil (§ RELIGIOUS IMAGERY).

Monster, Dragon, etc. ** A remote monstrous fear, beyond understanding, usually threatening from within rather than from the outside world.

The devouring monster: ** The 'jaws' of death. The dream may deal with man's continual quest for immortality.

If the dreamer gets the better of the monster: ** His triumph over his own fear of death, if the monster is an image of that fear.

** The most basic and primitive quality of life – the *prima materia* of alchemy – from which the individual must first free himself by conscious effort; though later he may be able to harness this force for specifically human purposes.

Cutting out the monster's heart or other vital organ, or lighting a fire inside it: ** The struggle against the dark forces of the underworld.

Winged dragon/dragon without wings: Spirit v. Earthly.

Man-eating monsters: * The insatiable hunger of the infant, and therefore exaggerated demands.

'All monsters and impossibilities are vain hopes of things which will not turn out' (Artemidorus).

Mouse * Mousey, diffident.

Otter Has some of the same significance as fishing (§ FISH) but in a primitive form: the unconscious content (the fish) are likely to be digested without ever being brought to dry land and the light of consciousness.

Parts of animals (the limbs, eyes, mouth, etc.): These usually have the same significance as parts of the human body (§ BODY). *If the four legs of an animal are particularly emphasized, possibly in contrast with a three-legged animal:* quaternity; or a whole rounded personality with all four functions of the mind (§) fully developed. *Tail:* ** Penis.

Pig or Wild Boar ** Ignorance, stupidity, selfishness, gluttony. It may be that the dreamer's better self is beginning to recognize these unattractive qualities in himself; without such recognition there can be no transformation or mastery of them.

Pigs and jewels: ** Pearls before swine, and the failure to appreciate spiritual values.

Swineherd: * The Prodigal Son, and a period of licentiousness and degradation which is drawing to a close.

Big litters of piglets: * Fruitfulness.

Sow: ** The Terrible Mother (§ ARCHETYPES).

Wild Boar: ** Elemental and destructive phallic power. The archetypal masculine principle, and therefore the negative Animus in a woman's dream (§ ARCHETYPES); more superficially, the dreamer may be confronted by her repressed incestuous desires. The rest of the dream should indicate whether the dreamer is evading an issue that should be confronted and dealt with more courageously, or whether the best that can be hoped for in the circumstances is to find adequate protection for the time being.

Prehistoric animals ** Something from the remote past, and therefore from childhood, which is emphasized by the dreamer's size (§) in relation to these monsters, which depict the giantlike proportions of adults seen through the eyes of a child.

** Primal darkness and chaos. The gross dinosaur flesh that has been refined into human form and flesh by the slow process of evolution and elimination.

Preoccupied animals *If the animals are too preoccupied to take much notice of the dreamer:* ** Narcissism, autoeroticism.

Rabbits ** Fertility: breeding like rabbits. * Intuition, because modern town-dwellers fail to differentiate between rabbits and hares in their dreams.

A white rabbit: May show the dreamer the gateway to an inner world as in *Alice in Wonderland.*

Rat ** The diseased, not only because rats carry plague, but also because they infest a house (§), which is an image of the body. They may depict something else that is physically repulsive or sexually obscene to the dreamer, or be images of his morbid outlook. * Somebody whom the dreamer unconsciously thinks of as a 'rat' – likely to be disloyal and leave the sinking ship first. * The devouring and therefore the Terrible Mother (§ ARCHETYPES).

Sheep ** The god-fearing, 'good sheep'. Also the passive and 'sheepish'.

Sheep/wolves, sheep/goats: Good v. evil (§ CONFLICT).

One of the most important elements in trying to understand a dream is to be able to relate it to the individual's waking life, to discover the points of contact: if Artemidorus still deserves a certain respect, it is because he was already doing this assiduously in the second century. A man who was hoping for a large inheritance came to him with a dream about shearing sheep. In the dream he left the sheep half shorn and carried off half the wool, which the dreamer himself interpreted as meaning that he would get half the inheritance. As it turned out, he got nothing at all, so Artemidorus concludes, empirically enough, that leaving a job half done in a dream is a bad omen.

Sinister animals ** The pressures from the unconscious are such that the dreamer doubts his ability to cope with them.

Snake *** Sexuality. The image of the snake is as complex as the problem of sexuality, which may strike like poison to destroy a man's life, or be transformed into the deepest and most satisfactory relationship possible on earth. Snake dreams usually occur when the dark instinctual levels of existence are rejected and repudiated by the conscious mind, which is then more threatened than ever by them. Only by accepting and assimilating the dark earthly and primitive side of our nature can we become mature human beings. Man is part beast and part angel, but those who only try to be angel may end up the worst beasts.

A snake twined around the body or a limb: ** Bondage, a slave to the passions.

A snake, or worm, leaving a corpse by its mouth: ** Coitus: and that eternal aspect of man which resides in his powers to procreate. Therefore the snake may signify the root of being, life itself, with its beginnings that cannot be traced, of indefinite size and shape, yet determining the size and shape of everything; the very energy and dynamic power that distinguishes the corpse from the living person.

With its tail in its mouth: Again, coitus and the eternal

principle, as above. Also the whole libido (§ SHAPES, Circle).
Being swallowed by a snake : ** 'The serpent of time consumes us' (§ EATING, Being eaten).
'*A snake in the grass*' : * Disloyalty, envy, calumny.

Perhaps because they signify the chain of life, or because they are deadly poisonous, snakes are also associated with the souls of the dead, with ancestors and the underworld of death as well as that of the unconscious.

** The principle of evil, the Collective Shadow (§ ARCHE-TYPES), the devil who seduced Eve in the serpent's guise.

* Fear, anguish, which may relate to an inner state of apprehension about all that is strange and has to be conquered; or to an actual danger that must be overcome.

Especially snake twined around a staff or a similar object:
* Healing, rebirth, renewal, possibly because the snake sloughs its skin and 'grows young again'; also because of the effect of the unconscious forces that may be released once the individual is no longer divided against himself.

* Wisdom: 'be wise as serpents'; a worldly cunning with which to match evil.

The colour of the snake may help pin down its significance (§ COLOURS).

Toad ** An ugly creature, and therefore whatever the individual considers ugly in his behaviour; abortions, especially because the toad has something in common with the embryo.
Toad/Eagle : Earthly v. spiritual values.

Transformation of animals Metamorphosis of the dreamer or other people into animals, animals into people, etc. (§ TRANSFORMATION, not Animals).

Unicorn ** The source of grace, which includes the idea of purity. It is a symbol of the herald of Christ, as well as of the Holy Spirit that conceived of the Virgin.

** The union of opposites (two horns symbolize conflict – § HORNS – so the unicorn has been interpreted as the resolution of that conflict), and the surge of renewed vitality when the tension and conflict are resolved.

Vermin *In the house* : may have the same significance as insects

(§) (like lice on the body) and refer to an unwanted pregnancy; parasites, small scurrying creatures, the patter of little feet, and therefore undesired children, whether progeny or younger brothers and sisters.

Vertebrates: lower: ** The Unconscious; higher: ** The emotions.

Wild animals Danger, whether dangerous passions within or dangerous people. ** Brute destructive force from the unconscious, threatening the safety of the individual. The instinct or drive must be prevented from becoming destructive and harmful. * Dangerous people. The parents may be depicted as frightening animals if the dreamer is in danger of depending too much on them; then the unconscious compensates for this by making them appear in their negative, terrifying aspect. * The embodiment of anxiety.

Domesticating wild animals: ** A veneer (only) of civilized behaviour; or else that fear has been overcome, at least superficially.

Wolf Alarming, swift-moving predator. ** The unrestricted, unsheltered and vicious; the diabolical inhabitant of the wilderness. Frequently used to portray cruel, sadistic fantasies without apparent responsibility on the part of the dreamer.

In winter and at night: The wolf is particularly vicious and dangerous, a night visitor of battlefields.

The she-wolf: * The harlot; but also known in myth and life to care for and suckle outcasts.

** The Terrible Mother (§ ARCHETYPES).

Wounded animals § WOUNDS.

APPETITES

Hunger or thirst: ** Sexual desire. All appetites are interchangeable in dreams, but usually some less embarrassing substitute serves as an image of sexual desire.

Sharing a meal with someone: ** A wish for intercourse with that person.

Stopping to drink at a fountain: ** The dreamer satisfying his sexual desire for a woman in fantasy (this would certainly be so if accompanied by an emission). (§ SEX).

Restaurants: * Brothels:

(§ EATING, DRINK, SEX, etc.)

ARCHETYPES There are three main ingredients of the individual's personality that appear in dreams as separate figures – sometimes as people the dreamer knows, sometimes as fictitious characters or personifications, more rarely as other images. The worst side of the individual has been called his Shadow and is the personification of his worst faults and weaknesses.

The Anima, or in the case of a woman, the Animus, is the embodiment of whatever is of the opposite sex within the dreamer: in a man it will be all that is feminine and emotional in him; in a woman it will be her masculine attributes. Finally there is the ideal or true Self, the highest potential that the individual is capable of attaining and that may communicate with him through his dreams. Although the Self starts as a vague figure of potential standing somewhere in the future, once the other two figures have been properly integrated into the personality, he may become the whole real many-sided Self. Once the dream figures have pointed to a reality that lies beyond them, they will have served their purpose and so be unlikely to appear in dreams again.

Because the chief quality of inner being is energy, each of these dream figures represents a different aspect of the vital forces at the individual's disposal, and each can galvanize this energy.

For the particular manifestations of the Archetypes, § PEOPLE (Hero, Old Man, Unknown Man, Unknown Woman, etc.); also ANIMALS, SHAPES, etc.

When approaching the archetypal figures, it is important to bear in mind the healthy person's final aim or goal: every aspect of the personality should thrive in its own domain without encroaching on the territory of the others; the continual conflict along the borders should temper and strengthen the character; and all the parts, having first been clearly differentiated and known, should ultimately become related to and integrated into the whole personality, the centre of which is the Self rather than the ego (though, confusingly, selfishness, self-interest, self-centredness, etc., are related more to the ego – egocentricity – and not the true Self.)

The Ego The 'I' of the dream. The ego is above all only a part of the Whole Self, and its conflict with other forces within the personality figures predominantly in dreams.

The most common abuse of the ego is for it to exaggerate its own separateness and engulf all other aspects of the Self. This leads to a rigid, distorted and materialistic outlook at the expense of what is equally real, though insubstantial – namely, the potential and spiritual realms. It also leads to egotism, difficulty in trusting others or relating to them, and too little loving acceptance. This onesidedness can be compensated for by making as much room as possible for dreams or any manifestations of the unconscious.

At the other extreme, the ego, which is basically the elaborate receptive organ for assessing reality (whether conscious or unconscious), may be in danger of being swallowed up by the ubiquitous dream state. It must be preserved against this regressive urge by objective self-criticism, differentiation of the unconscious by constant observation, as well as attention, conscientiousness and patience, all of which strengthen the ego.

Every person sprang from an anonymous unity with Nature (in the womb) and must return to it, but with a difference: to be pure nature, but conscious of it. Therefore, consciousness must defend its reason without letting the imagination and unconscious atrophy.

Normally, to achieve the proper and realistic balance, the sacrifice of the ego is required, for the ego is full of delusions and limitations, unable to see beyond its own standpoint and outlook to the reality of the Other.

The Shadow (a figure of the same sex as the dreamer) *The person whom the dreamer fails to recognize; a vague instinct figure, sometimes standing slightly behind the dreamer*. The neglected side of the individual, that part of his potential that he never developed; sides of his character that have already been thwarted and frustrated; but above all, aspects never recognized.

Everybody has his individual Shadow, and it is nearly always the worst side of himself that he has failed to recognize. It is a rare exception for somebody to have such a dingy conscious view of himself that his Shadow is the personification of his better side. The sensitive altruist will have a brutal egotistic Shadow; the courageous individual will have a cowardly Shadow; the ever-loving person will have a bitter cantankerous Shadow; Dr Jekyll had Mr Hyde, and so on.

The encounter with the Shadow is usually painful: the shock of seeing ourselves as we really are at our worst. To face it humbly is to accept ourselves, and from that to see the rest of reality as it is. It is the way to greater understanding of others, new insights, particularly into the unconscious. It often revives normal instincts, appropriate reactions, creative impulses that have been condemned to conscious oblivion along with the evil and destructive sides of the personality.

It is important both to know the enemy and to cultivate and channel this vital energy that may otherwise erupt in a primitive and dangerous manner.

Think of the person you detest most in the world, mix in the worst characteristics of anyone else you know, and you have a fair idea of your own Shadow. It frequently appears in dreams in the image of people whom the dreamer dislikes or envies in waking life.

The dark side of ourselves is not destroyed by being ignored. On the contrary, it continues to seethe and fester below the surface, and normally requires little more than a change of circumstances to become only too apparent. One of the most obvious ways for people to reveal these inner qualities is by their obsessive and overemotional dislike of the same qualities in other people. To withdraw these 'projections', to recognize the inner conflict from which they arise, is one of the major works of maturing.

There are many stories about mistaking these projections for reality, attacking them and being destroyed by the resulting strife, war, etc., in the outside world, and by madness (paranoia) in the inner world.

Extrovert/Introvert. The value of integrating the Shadow into the personality is perhaps clearest in the case of the extrovert and introvert. When the time comes to develop the other side, which has so far been neglected, then dreams call attention to this.

Trying to live a whole life focused exclusively on the outside world or devoted entirely to the inner realm inevitably limits the scope of the individual's life and leads to many delusions. For the introvert to break out into the world of sun and trees, and for the extrovert to begin to reckon with his inner disposition, his own needs, etc., is for both a fresh experience that broadens their horizons and incidentally gives them a greater understanding of each other.

If the individual neglects to do this, it will not only exclude him from the other realm, but he will also find himself becoming increasingly incompetent in the sphere to which he has exclusively limited himself. Even the extrovert's relationship with the outside world will begin to play him false because he can't reckon with inner factors. Similarly, the introvert's conflict with the outside world will disturb even his inner tranquillity.

Anima/Animus (a figure of the opposite sex to the dreamer) It is common knowledge that young people usually fall in love first with their own idea of a woman/man, and they project this idea on to a likely face and get a shock when the person beyond that face turns out to be very different from their idea. This feminine figure within the man and masculine figure within the woman have been called the Anima and Animus; they play many other roles throughout a person's life besides the one just mentioned. This confusion of the inner realm with the outside world can be a cause of strife throughout life, not only between wife and husband, but also between mother-in-law and son-in-law, and so on.

Later in life this inner potential of androgyny may be neglected and abused with one of two results. Either the individual will become cut off from the necessary influence of elements of the opposite sex (a woman, for example, may become hysterically emotional while a man may become increasingly dry). Or in certain circumstances the inferior function may take possession of the individual. Then the man may behave like a second-rate woman, becoming sentimental, capricious, unstable; whereas the woman may become avid for authority, make intellectual assertions or become quarrelsome.

Ideally, if we come to terms with the Anima and Animus – recognize them for what they are throughout life – they are the source of our understanding of the opposite sex, as well as key figures in opening up the full range and potential of our inner being; and they enable us to reconcile intellect with feeling.

Anima This is the centre and pattern of all the feminine forces within the man. The emotional, intuitive and instinctive side of his nature. All the women the individual has known in his life – but especially his mother – will have helped to form his image of what is feminine. In his dreams this female figure may have features of any of them, or may be a completely unknown woman, or be represented by such animals as have been feminine deities in mythology.

Increasing awareness of this feminine principle enables the individual to integrate his spontaneous, receptive, sensitive and adaptable qualities, but above all to develop the warmth and genuine feeling in him – all of which will compensate for his aggressive male conscious attitudes.

There are four main aspects of the feminine figure, which in a woman's dreams represent her Self, each with a positive and a negative side – though usually it is the negative side that first reveals itself in dreams (§ a woman's SELF, below).

Dreams attempt to compensate for lopsided conscious attitudes. Therefore the Anima usually appears when a man is neglecting the feminine side of himself and before the consequences of this have been felt. This may mean that the individual is forcing everything in him into the masculine mould, which will by degrees turn tenderness into cruelty, obedience into defiance, sensitive tendencies into hatred.

Especially during the second half of life the failure to respect and assimilate these vital feminine forces within often leads to premature crustiness, rigidity and obstinacy; or else weariness and irresponsibility, often accompanied by a tendency to drink.

Alternatively, the repressed feminine characteristics may erupt in irrational moodiness, and so on.

Neglect of the Anima can affect his relations with women in various ways. Apart from projecting his own image of women on to an actual woman and thus failing to see her as she really is – and incidentally cutting him off from other large chunks of reality – the woman concerned will tend in response to identify with the man's expectations and hence to play-act, leading to a spiral of bogusness.

On the other hand, if a man's impression of women, formed in particular circumstances, has rendered his Anima repellent to him, he may project this figure on to every other woman, and so find no escape from his fear of women.

Sometimes a man projects his Anima on to one unobtainable person, thereby avoiding contact with the opposite sex altogether.

In these and other ways the Anima, instead of being the guide, becomes the siren of daydream and fantasy, wrecking real relationships, obscuring the true qualities of the other person, a fatal and destructive succubus who creates an illusion of androgynous self-sufficiency.

The Anima reveals her inner wisdom only to the man who grapples seriously with her, knowing her for what she is, treating her attentively and considerately, but also with discipline. Only then will she guide him to the full range of his personality, his potential, his true Self. By accepting her as an independent inner personality to whom he can relate, a man transforms the Anima into an ally, just as with a woman.

Animus This represents the masculine features in a woman's character which, integrated properly, will give her greater discernment, self-knowledge, and ability to reflect and deliberate. Although it is an inherent part of the woman's potential, it is affected and formed by her contacts with men and is completely different for each individual, varying as much as men themselves – from the highest to the lowest, hero to rake. If it is developed into a whole balanced personality in its own right, the Animus is the natural guide to the deepest layers of the mind.

The Animus usually appears in a woman's dreams to remind her of the need to develop these masculine characteristics in herself. Because this archetype is the source of a woman's judgement and convictions, these are in danger of remaining at a primitive stage if. it is neglected: the woman is then gullible to rigid collective convictions appropriated without a thought; unquestioned conventional opinions, assumptions that have originally belonged to her family and that have been taken over wholesale and never examined.

If her negative Animus later begins to dominate her life – usually when the man in her life has let her down – she may become devastatingly obstinate and opinionated, sure that she is always right in everything: everybody 'ought' and 'should' do this and that, however irrational, because 'I just know...'

The more the image of the Animus recurs in the dreams, the more urgent it will be to develop this masculine and intellectual side of her being and relate to it, without losing touch with her true nature – the necessary feminine antidote to this prejudiced and argumentative side of herself, which necessarily remains unrelated to the real needs of others.

Like the Anima, the Animus may be projected on to someone else with ensuing disillusionment: a woman expects from the man she lives with something that is really part of herself, and that has nothing to do with him. This indicates an immaturity in the woman, who will often still be attached to her mother in an infantile way.

Although of course it is usual for the male partner to express the male attitudes in a family, the woman is able to share in them all the more fully for recognizing them in herself.

Through dreams one can come to know the particular idio-syncrasies of one's personal and individual Anima or Animus and allow for it in waking life. The dream may reflect the conflict of Logos (intellect, conscious spirit) v. Eros (emotions, and unconscious soul). Only when the proper balance between these is found will the way be paved for the integration of the whole character. (§ A Man's SELF, below. The four main aspects of this will apply to the Animus, which may be made up of those particular faculties that complement a woman's qualities and correspond to the Shadow side of herself.)

The Self While the Shadow and the Anima/Animus are those parts of a dreamer's potential that have been neglected so that the main characteristics of the personality can be realized, the Self is the archetype of the future, the potential development of the individual. It is like a figure beckoning from the future, necessarily of the same sex as the dreamer, but later becoming a symbol of wholeness including all aspects of his personality, past and future, active and passive, creative and receptive.

The symbols themselves may range from the highest to the lowest. Almost anything may serve as a symbol, but it will be easily recognizable as referring to the inner being because of the immense significance the dreamer attaches to it. Captain Ahab's quest for the white whale is an example of the quest for the Self, albeit in its negative, destructive aspect.

The Self is the higher spiritual man, the unknown and even unknowable quality of human nature itself, in its godlike universal and eternal aspect and in its individuality in time. The finite limited man, reaching out for the roots of his being – which are both his source and his goal – transcends the personal to embrace the whole range of nature and reality to its very depths. In a potential wholeness, which becomes the image of God within him, this unity is achieved by penetrating the sphere of inner being, which at the same time will permeate the worldly sphere of unique individual existence. In this way the potential self becomes the actual self; the seed grows into the whole integrated personality.

When the images of this archetype start cropping up in dreams, it will probably mark the beginning of the process of becoming whole, identifying with something other than our everyday selves, and also more enduring. This peculiarly intimate knowledge and experience of reality makes it spring into being in such a way that what lies beyond the ego becomes as vivid as personal experience; indeed, it so becomes personal experience that there is a danger of confusing the image of reality, the clear glass, the godlike, with the reality.

If the images of the archetypes appear in their negative, destructive form, which they often do at first, it will indicate that their particular forces are being neglected and so turned to a disadvantage. Just as the Tarot cards that are upside down are supposed to point to what can be altered most easily and turned to good advantage, a negative archetype indicates the very point at which there is most hope of advance, of change for the better within the character.

There are four main aspects of the woman's Self and of the man's Self, and each is related to one of the four functions of the mind (§); and the Self becomes whole when all the different aspects have been separately developed and then finally integrated within the one individual, thus:

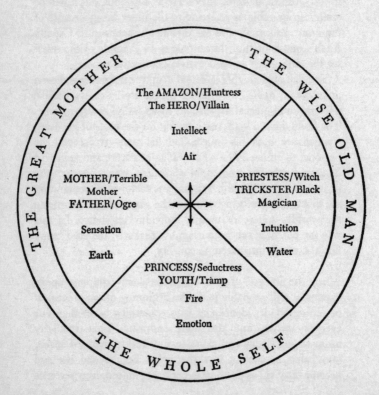

A Woman's Self Every woman is the realm of feminine energy incarnate. She embodies the intangibles of feeling and instinct. This is the archetype of nature and of life, the earthy and the erotic.

There are four main aspects of the feminine potential, which are related to the four functions of the mind (§): the Mother, sensation; the Princess, emotion; the Amazon, intellect; the Priestess, intuition. Just as the feminine realm compensates for the driving conscious will of the male world in a general way, so the particular type of the woman's femininity will complement the man: the effeminate emotional man with an amazonlike female counterpart is not uncommon.

The Great Mother. Mother Earth This archetype is the equivalent of the Wise Old Man, and represents wholeness in the woman or potential wholeness. It mustn't be confused with that of the feminine potential which is motherhood, the Mother (see below).

Although actually bearing children may help to develop the motherly aspect of the character, it isn't really necessary, because this aspect of the personality is in fact inner and spiritual, and may be cultivated in many other ways. The character can become whole, integrate all the different aspects of womanhood, in almost any circumstances; and it can also fail to do so however favourable the circumstances.

1. *The Mother*. This is the protective maternal aspect of woman: her domestic qualities of making a home, nourishing, sheltering, being loving and gentle. Because this is the collective social aspect of womanhood, the general attitude has overemphasized its importance – at the expense of the personal and individual flowering of the woman, without which she can't even be much of a mother.

Although it is important for the woman to discover and develop the main part of her potential, it is equally important that she does not neglect the two subsidiary aspects of her true Self; and ultimately it will be through concentrating on her inferior, that is, the least considered, side of herself, that she can become whole. There will always be considerable conflict between what is expected of her socially (the communal anthill or the social strait-jacket) and the cultivation of her inner potential, by concentrating on the other three aspects of her true Self.

The Terrible Mother. This is the possessive, entwining, devouring and destructive side of motherhood, which may arise as a result of the over-protective understanding mother suddenly threatening the individual's growth, development and independence. The mother who keeps her children tied to her, with unnatural love and devotion, may appear to the children in this form in their dreams; or she may even dream of herself in this form, grunting like a pig or howling like a wolf, etc.

Alternatively, the dream may depict the terrifying aspect of the actual mother in childhood; she may be shown in this form as a protection against incest, revealing the desire for it as well as the fear of it.

The archetype of the Terrible Mother is also the angry goddess, who has given birth to all the abominations of the world, everything wicked and unclean.

The mother who is nothing-but-a-mother, and neglects her other qualities, is the most likely to be revealed in this terrifying aspect in the end.

2. *The Princess.* This quality in a woman is the very basis of love and personal relationship. It is the girl, the flirt; the eternally youthful quality of spontaneity and warmth that can continue to develop alongside other, more mature aspects. It is the power not only to attract, but to be attracted, and as long as it is the stimulus behind a conscious choice, it need not be disruptive – even though it retains its essential nature, which is its individual and highly subjective approach to other people.

The Seductress. Favours historic costume in dreams, preferably Greek or Roman: She is the fatal siren, the wrecker of marriages, the succubus and image of erotic fantasy, which prevents real relationship as the result of highflown dreams on a closed egotistical circuit.

3. *The Amazon.* This is the personification of the intellectual qualities in a woman. If it is the main aspect of a woman's

character, she will be a career woman, the companion of men and the competer with them. But it is often the inferior part of her that, if neglected, will require drastic consideration later in life.

The Huntress. Epitomizes that type of career woman who hounds men either because she is frustrated in her own ambitions, which she has then projected on to a particular man or on to men in general, or else because she has failed to develop other important sides of her femininity, or both.

4. *The Priestess.* Intuition is not particularly favoured by modern society, so this aspect of womanhood has found particularly little outlet. As a main function it must be almost extinct, but those women who do manage to cultivate it are all the more remarkable for being rare.

The inner world is as much a part of reality and of creation as the tangible world, which can be perceived subjectively only by the senses. By disparaging intuition and the inner realm that is experienced directly by the mind – a far finer mechanism than the eye or the ear – we lose contact with the most obvious and immediate alternative view of reality, which could act as a balance to the egotistical lopsided view, which so easily mistakes the world as the ego sees it for reality, the world as it really is.

The Witch or Sorceress. A primitive undeveloped intuition cuts a woman off from the whole spiritual sphere and is unreliable when she does make use of it; she may become trapped in a world of subjective visions that cannot be related to anyone or anything else.

The witch, as a figure in dreams, may refer to any of the negative aspects of Womanhood, especially the Terrible Mother. Her magical intuitive powers would have to be stressed to indicate this archetype: she might behave like a female version of the Trickster/Black Magician.

These four aspects of womanhood, each with its negative shadowy side, are likely to act as patterns of influence within the individual character; a proper balance should be maintained between the four so that each can develop and mature in its own sphere.

Only rarely does one Archetype take over the whole personality – with disastrous results.

Many of these features and characteristics of the Feminine Potential may apply to a man's Anima.

A Man's Self This is the embodiment of the principle of Logos, intellect, conscious spirit. In primitive tribes this spirit is far less highly developed than in civilized man and is all too apt to be swallowed up in the unconscious again. But equally, the civilized man is inclined to over-discriminate, become hypercritical and lead himself astray into an arid intellectual waste. This process, which has taken place over many generations of evolution, is reflected again in each individual growing up from the womb and total at-oneness with nature, to the eventual break with the mother.

It is a question not of disparaging this great prize of conscious intellect, but of reintegrating the unconscious realm when the time is right. Just as never leaving the mother is quite different from leaving the mother and then getting married, so in the inner realm discriminating all that is truly masculine is necessary before the conscious principle can be related to the unconscious and not submerged in it in a regressive way. The dangers of this are often depicted in dreams.

The Wise Old Man This is the common archetype for the whole of the man's Self, in all its aspects; his potential beckoning him from the future, but above all, of those vital forces which comprise the conscious spirit. When admiration for his superiors (and especially his father) begins to flag – when their ideas no longer seem adequate – the Wise Old Man may appear in dreams as a sign of the wisdom and superiority that the individual would like to acquire for himself.

None of the archetypal figures can be mustered by one's own resources, but the Wise Old Man often appears when the individual, or the hero of the dream, is in a hopeless and desperate situation from which only the spirit can extricate him, often galvanizing reserves of energy from the unconscious in order to do so. He is often the source of inspiration and enthusiasm, insight and understanding, as well as determination. If he gives advice, it should usually be taken.

As with the Woman's Self, there are four main aspects of the Man's Self, each corresponding to one of the functions of the Mind (§): the Father, sensation; the Eternal Youth, emotion; the Hero, intellect; the Magician, intuition.

1. *The Father.* This figure is the embodiment of authority, law, order, social conventions, patterns of behaviour, etc., as well as masculine protectiveness. The actual father will have contributed considerably to forming this father-image in the individual.

The Ogre. *** The oppressive father, who threatens individuality with the mould of conformity. Any problems the individual has with regard to discipline, whether he is rebellious or oversubmissive, can usually be referred back to the relationship with the actual father, but if he can recognize the Father Archetype in himself (including the potential father that he may one day be); if he can see the problem as in himself, where he has considerably more control over it, he should be able to turn the negative and destructive aspect of this archetype into something positive – as long as it can be seen in proportion as one of four main elements in his own personality.

2. *The Youth.* This is the male equivalent of the Princess, and because of its youth contains within itself the seed of potential growth into the Hero and ultimately the Wise Old Man, embodying all aspects of the Self; for he is also the Seeker.

The Tramp. The wanderer, the drifter (who has been known to collect driftwood in a dream): Without any other influence this aspect of the vital forces within shuns all commitment, refuses to mature, and ends up a boy, pickled by old age, rather than embracing manhood.

The Hunter : An inquisitive love of adventure in contrast with patience, self-sacrifice and devotion.

3. *The Hero/Villain.* The daring and initiative of the individual, his will and driving force. This aggressive male attitude has been so adulated in all spheres that it isn't usually hard to

observe the direction and outlet this particular vital force is finding for itself, even though the trend be antiheroic on the surface. The Messiah, the Saviour, is the most exalted manifestation of this aspect of the Self. May be represented by the Healer, appearing in sanctuaries or caves.

The Villain. Being the unconscious root or counterpart of the conscious intellect and ego, this Archetype has a tendency to egoism that may amount to megalomania – especially if the emotions are neglected. If the individual identifies with this particular force within the Self (or if on the contrary he so neglects it that in certain circumstances it erupts and takes possession of his personality), his disregard for the unconscious feminine realm within himself and his lack of respect for other people will inevitably warp his actions, however grandiose and lofty his expressed intentions. These are the circumstances in which the idea of the resurrection and afterlife are used as a weapon to torture and massacre people; even love has been wielded in various ways, just as a blanket can be used to smother people. This truly aggressive and self-assertive aspect of man can adapt almost anything into another weapon in the arms dump.

4. *The Trickster/Black Magician.* This figure is as elusive as intuition itself. Its dark and light sides seem much less clearly differentiated than in the others; he may start out helpful and then turn nasty, or vice versa. At the end of the quest, however, when the difficulties have been met and the obstacles overcome, when the hardships and chores imposed by this figure and the period of trying to get out of its clutches but eventually remaining willingly have ended, all the efforts are invariably rewarded, whatever has happened meanwhile.

ASCENDING ** Development and increase, possibly within the mind or in the sexual sphere. May refer specifically to erection or to waking up – the waking state in contrast with sleep.
Ascending and descending in a lift: ** Coitus, towards which the dreamer has a somewhat mechanical attitude (§ BUILDINGS, Lift).

44

ASHES * An act of abasement, whether the sackcloth and ashes of contrition, or being belittled and humiliated involuntarily. * That which endures after the fire, namely, the spirit.

ATTITUDES *What seems to be the dreamer's attitude in the dream* cannot be trusted; usually bogus. It is often just a charade, a pose, adopted in order to conceal real feelings, which are in fact better revealed by the action of the dream (§ ACTION) and the underlying emotion accompanying the dream (§ EMOTIONS). The dreamer may adopt this bogus attitude in order to avoid apparent responsibility for the action of the dream, salve his conscience, or express the other side of his inner conflict.

BAG * A woman: 'the old bag'.

BALL ** Testicles: 'balls'.
Playing with the ball, ball games: ** Playing with the testicles, therefore erection.
Kicking the ball: ** Erection, as above, or fear of castration (§).
If the ball goes off at an angle: * Misdirected sexual excitement, perhaps not inspired by the dreamer's wife.
** Breast or pregnant belly.
** Circle, and therefore wholeness (§ SHAPES).
A golden ball in the dark, in the depths: * The glimmering of inner light to illuminate the unconscious.

BANK ** Emotional, rather than financial, capital and security.
Vaults: * The womb, or the store of semen.

BEHEADING ** Losing one's head, therefore losing one's mind, possibly as the result of failing to cultivate its potential at the right time (§ MIND), or at least the fear of this.
** Divorcing the head from the heart: for example, becoming too career-conscious at the expense of personal relationships.
** One part of the body may stand for another (§BODY), and therefore fear of castration or impotence (§ CASTRATION).

BELLS *Alarm bells especially:* ** Conscience, warning the dreamer.

BIRDS ** Imagination: 'flights of fancy', or thoughts, ideas, which also 'fly' about the room, or back and forth.

In a cage or with broken wings: ** The imagination hemmed in or mutilated by circumstances, drudgery, and so on.

Clipping the wings: * Restraint, mortification, possibly of wild or fanciful but obsolete notions and values, in which case the clipping will be a necessary preliminary to the next phase.

** Aspirations, especially the spirit soaring towards the celestial, the Divine.

†: *Birds with wings/An unfledged or plucked bird, or an earthbound creature:* ** Spiritual aspirations v. corporeal or material considerations. In alchemy the monster, the earthbound dragon (signifying the *prima materia*) is transformed into the eagle, the goose of Hermes, or the Peacock.

** Women: 'birds'.

In a man's dream: ** The Anima.

In a woman's dream: ** The Self.

White/black birds: ** The two aspects of the Anima or Self, the black bird signifying the dark, neglected, or shadowy side (§ ARCHETYPES, the Anima, the Self).

* Liberty: 'free as a bird'.

If the bird was a pet: The general idea may be modified by personal considerations, emotions. The dreamer's childhood aspirations, for example, and what became of them.

A display of plumage: * Social refinements, or the individual's persona, façade (§ CLOTHES).

Golden-winged bird: May have the same significance as fire (§).

A high-flying bird or possibly a bird living in the upper storeys of a building: * Soaring to the heights, through awareness; a creature that can tell of the kingdom of heaven.

Chicken ** A bird that cannot fly, and therefore the imagination made to serve a utilitarian function. If the chickens are being kept for their eggs (§), there will be more hope of future potential growth than if they are being kept for meat.

Even when the dream isn't explicit on such subjects, the individual on waking may be able to discover the possible fate of the creatures simply by trying to visualize it.

Cock: ** Lust: the 'cock'.

Somebody turning into a chicken: ** The dreamer's unconscious believes that person, possibly himself (§ PEOPLE), to be a coward.

Crow **Priest, who also wears black (§ COLOURS) and buries the dead, therefore death.

Dove ** The Anima (§ ARCHETYPES).

Eagle ** Perceptiveness: 'eagle-eyed'. Awareness. A lofty flight of the mind or spirit. The male spirit of enthusiasm. ** Domination.
If the dreamer identifies with the eagle: ** His own wish to dominate. But if the dream is accompanied by anguish or dread, then this will-to-dominate may be threatening some other, more sensitive side of the dreamer's nature.
If the dreamer feels threatened: ** Somebody else's will to dominate him.

Owl ** The departed soul of somebody who is dead, represented by the bird's ghostly night-time appearance and eerie cry. Also wisdom; or the Anima (§ ARCHETYPES).

Peacock ** The unfolding realization of wholeness, because of the appearance of all the colours in its feathers and the circular shape of its fanned-out tail (§ SHAPES, Circle). Also rebirth and resurrection, dying in order to live; in alchemy the peacock has much the same significance as the phoenix, rising renewed from the ashes. It also plays an important role in Gnosticism; and the Pope used to be crowned with peacock feathers.
** Male beauty. The dreamer may have a particular beautiful man in mind.

Phoenix ** Rebirth, resurrection.

Raven ** The Devil, who is also black and winged. A sinister aspect of the father image. The Shadow: the first dark confused phase of knowing the inner realm (§ ARCHETYPES).

Wild Goose *Can move on land, water and in the air:* ** The soul. Geese are the outlawed pagan divinities of nature, and traditionally the companions of witches.

BIRTH It is conceivable that the experience, and often shock, of being born registers in the unconscious and features in dreams, in symbolic form, whenever some similar confrontation with life stirs up memories in the depths of the mind which have never been consciously apprehended.

The images for being born may or may not be reversed; the dreamer may thus crawl out of small holes or into small holes, come out of or go into the sea, go along narrow canals in a small boat, into or out of tunnels, etc. Such dreams are apt to add considerable needless anxiety to the present situation, which in reality has very little to do with an event that was over and done with ages ago. Therefore, it is quite an advantage to be able to recognize such dreams and contemplate them, bearing firmly in mind that it happened then: however painful the experience, it is of the past. (In *New Approaches to Dream Interpretation*, Nandor Fodor offers considerable evidence to substantiate the idea: details of the dream were verified with details of the actual birth as supplied by the mother.)

A Birth
Happening or about to happen in the dream: ** Rebirth, regeneration. The wish to elevate one's life or repeat it without the same mistakes. This theme of enlightenment and renewal – the truth remaining valid through change – becomes particularly meaningful towards the end of the dreamer's life, and is more likely to crop up in dreams then: youth grows old, beauty fades, heat cools, brightness dims, but the original spark of life that generated them is infinite and eternal.
An embryo: ** A life that as yet lacks scope or is being stifled in some way.

BITING
Even when it looks like a frightening attack: ** An act of love

(§ AGGRESSION). The teeth (the active male component) enter the flesh (the female). Simultaneously the attacked enters the mouth of the attacker. There may of course be a sadistic undercurrent to the love.

* 'Getting one's teeth into something'.

BODY *** The individual, whether the dreamer or somebody else, as a whole: his personality and mind as well as his body, just as the body is in fact an outward manifestation of the inner person, but especially his ego (§ ARCHETYPES). As the basic frame of reference for all experience, the body is the original source and fund of symbols.

The child's first conscious realization of the world is through the body and its functions, which recur later in dreams as symbols of this encounter. For the child the body is also a cipher for the unfathomable, which is why much unconscious material expresses itself in body symbolism.

The upper part of the body: *** The mind; the spiritual and platonic aspects of the character.

The lower part of the body: *** The instincts.

An adult's head on a child's body: ** Somebody, probably the dreamer, who is mentally but not sexually mature.

†: *Upper part/lower part:* ** Mind v. instincts.

The right side of the body: ** The upright moral side of the person concerned.

The left side, including left hand, left foot, etc.: ** The immoral, inferior, undeveloped aspects of the character. The Shadow (§ ARCHETYPES).

One part of the body may represent another: But as is usual in dreams, one significant or embarrassing part is represented by something less embarrassing.

Anything pointed, such as finger, arm, tooth: *** The penis.

Any normal opening in the body, such as the mouth, but also a hole in the body: ** The anus or the vagina.

A hole in the back or in the back of the hand, etc.: ** The anus; *a hole in the front:* ** the vagina.

There is a tendency in dreams for displacement to occur from below upward; therefore it is important to see if anything that happens to the chest, the head, etc., would make more sense if applied to the genital region. *Similarly, the functions of the body are interchangeable, so that secretions such as mucus, tears, urine :* ** Semen. *Holding the breath :* * Stool retention.

Abdomen (stomach, belly) ** The place of repressed feelings, emotions (§), especially *angst*.

Becoming fat ** Pregnancy. Fear of pregnancy may be transferred into fear of becoming fat.

Anus (excrement) ** The first infantile experiences of self-expression and self-assertion; it has become a symbol in dreams of ego power. This may be positive and indicate self-reliance – a legitimate reaction against herd conformism – when the community has become the destructive deperson-alized mother; the combative and martial qualities of the ego, which may in the circumstances be necessary for survival. More likely the dream will refer to an arrested egotism, self-will and defiance.
Excrement : ** Something dirty: dirty behaviour, egotistical pleasure. Also dirty fighting, egotistical strife. The dream may be trying to indicate to the individual in striking imagery how egotistical, childish, rebellious and antisocial his demands are. *If the excrement is transformed into (or replaced by) living animals, possibly rats :* ** The individual is beginning to master his regressive impulses.
** Money.
Playing with it : ** Anxiety about money, as well as the fear of responsibility.
Constipation (in life as well as in dreams) : *** Reluctance to part with this symbol of money: avarice. The *Assyrian Dream Book* claims that eating faeces will bring wealth to the dreamer.
*The original raw material from which the world and man was created. Matter in contrast with Spirit. The earth, the realm of the feminine, and therefore the Great Mother (§ ARCHETYPES). The realm of feeling.

Everything has a positive side to which the dreamer can turn. In order to develop emotionally and overcome repressed feelings (which are probably the cause of his arrestedness), the dreamer can relate to the realm of feeling. In order to overcome the Terrible Mother (who may be warping and stunting his growth), he can relate to the Great Mother.

Evacuation : ** Being delivered of worries and responsibilities, being purged of guilt and repressions, or being liberated from inhibitions. * The sexual act. * 'Verbal diarrhoea'.

Not only was excrement supposed to contain the basic raw material from which the alchemists were to make gold, but de Becker points out the tenuous but possible (?) relationship between Luther's anal fixation and the capital exploitation for which the Protestants were mainly responsible.

Blood ** Menstruation (§ WOUNDS). * The blood of Christ, and therefore the life of the spirit as well as the body. Especially lamb's or hare's blood or blood mixed with water: communion. * 'Blood brothers': the spirit of unity.
Bath of blood : * Baptism into maturity and manhood.
* A vital substance, therefore semen. *Bloodsucking :* * Sucking out semen; causing an emission.

Eye *** The observing and discriminating eye of consciousness; the mind. The 'eye of God' and the 'eye of eternity'. The realm of the masculine: the man's Self and the woman's Animus (§ ARCHETYPES). It is the prototype of the mandala (§ SHAPES).
Loss of eyesight : ** Loss of insight and enlightenment; loss of one eye will indicate partial loss. Also loss of sexual potency.
Regaining eyesight : * Regaining the innate wisdom of the child; rebirth (§ SUN, which has much the same significance).
* That which receives light: the open, the receptive, and therefore the feminine.
Something stuck in the eye : ** Coitus.

Hair ** Pubic hair: virility.
Baldness, hair being cut, etc.: ** Loss of virility, strength: impotence (§ CASTRATION). An unreasonable fear, and therefore a fear arising from the unconscious, often has a symbolic significance. Hence fears of going bald and so on could have more to do with anxiety about one's virility.

Hands ** The phallus. Also the ability to make things with one's hands; creativity.

The two hands contrasted with each other, a different object in each hand, etc.: ** On the one hand, and on the other – and the conflict between the two. The less acceptable of the alternatives will be in the left hand (§ POSITION).

A huge hand, especially from the sky, etc.: * 'The hand of God'.

Head ** The dreamer's conscious intentions. *A blow to the head:* * Those intentions receiving a blow.

Limbs *Any limb:* ** The male member, the phallus.

In a man's dream, loss of a limb: ** Castration (§).

In a woman's dream, loss of any part of the body that is irreplaceable, an eyelid, for example: ** Loss of virginity.

In the dream of a Jewish person, loss of some part of the body: * Circumcision, and being Jewish.

Being dismembered: ** The individual's life is breaking up or is in pieces, falling apart at the seams. This may be the necessary preparation for recentring in a new reality (cf. EARTHQUAKE).

Two limbs: * Brother and sister.

Mouth ** The receptive, but also the demanding. The grasping, in the sense of grabbing or understanding and absorbing. The dream may point to the needs of the individual. ** The feminine: yielding, kissing, female genitalia.

Nose ** Intuition. 'I smell something fishy, wrong' (§ MIND). Note: Dogs or other animals that are particularly well known for their ability to scent may be used especially to indicate this function. ** The penis.

Penis *** The phallic or sexual aspects of its activities (§ SEX).

Urine: *** An infantile form of sexuality. The first childish outpouring, which later develops into sexuality: Havelock Ellis points out that young children sometimes want to show their love by urinating on a beloved person. Latent sexuality, and therefore emotion: 'To gush with emotion'. The kidneys are known as 'the spring of feeling'.

The dream may indicate whether the individual is yielding too much to his emotions, or bottling them up.

* Inward purging, purification, by water pouring through the system (§ WATER).

* Talking: 'gushing' with words, etc.

Skin ** The individual's façade or persona; has much the same significance as clothing (§).

Hard, tough skin: ** The individual is presenting a hard, tough exterior to the world, but has so identified with that façade that he can no longer take it off (like clothes); he has become 'thick-skinned'.

Teeth *Teeth falling out:* *** The two periods when teeth do fall out: The loss of milk teeth, and therefore all problems relating to maturing, taking on responsibility, in contrast with remaining childish. *Teeth coming out easily:* ** Leaving childhood behind.

*** Old age. Becoming helpless or impotent; ineffectual: 'toothless'. *Especially if one is anxious about the teeth dropping out:* ** Fear of getting old, undesirable, etc., as above, or anxiety about maturing.

** A regressive wish: to be helpless as a baby, which has no teeth, and is free from sex troubles.

In women's dreams, especially if the teeth are swallowed: ** Conceiving a child: the mouth referring to the vagina and the stomach to the womb.

If the dreamer is relieved: * Something putrid, rotten, has finally been removed.

Teeth: ** Aggressive sexuality (§ BITING).

Drilling teeth may signify coitus, the drilling being the relevant factor while the teeth are merely incidental.

Tongue ** Penis. 'Holding the tongue': * Keeping a secret or failing to do so.

Womb § WOMB.

BOOKS *Especially notebooks:* ** Memories.

BOX ** A coffin, and therefore death (§) and death wishes. Freud thought a box might signify the womb, but chiefly because of a similarity in the German word. Nevertheless, death and the womb are linked symbolically, and both are places to retreat to when the dreamer is unwilling to face some grim aspect of his life.
** Some aspect of the dreamer's life which is being confined – in the box, boxed-in – by inner restrictions or outside forces.

BREAK *Especially breaking china or glass:* ** The breaking of something else in the dreamer's life which is fragile – 'shattered' ideals, 'broken' faith, etc. – which is often the result of a lack of equilibrium. (The custom of breaking a glass or a plate at a wedding is to ward off this type of misfortune.)
Breaking a staff or sceptre: ** Change, especially in relation to the sexual drives, symbolized by the staff. Breaking up of things as they are at present. It may be possible to turn what is unavoidable into a conscious sacrifice.

BRIDGE ** A crossing (§): a transition between two periods in the dreamer's life; a way across, using the conscious mind (in contrast with a way through via the unconscious, which would be signified by a tunnel). * Phallus: joining two bodies.

BUILDINGS Most buildings in dreams have much the same significance as the house, as well as much the same features: windows, doors, etc.

The House *** The human body and personality. Just as a man is often identified with his house, which is supposed to reveal his character, so in dreams the house often represents the dreamer.
Anything in the house: ** Something in the dreamer.
Someone else in the house: ** Some unrecognized aspect of the dreamer's character.
The front of the house: ** The dreamer's façade, or the 'front' he presents to the world.

Outside the house: ** A realm beyond the limits of what is personal: everything outside the dreamer.

†: *Going into/out of the house:* ** Being an introvert v. being extrovert.

The openings in the house (windows, doors, etc.): May correspond to the openings in the body.

Upstairs, rooms upstairs, including loft, attic, etc.: ** The brain or conscious mind.

The lower part, including basement, cellars, etc.: ** The instincts and the unconscious.

†: *Lectures or discussions may take place upstairs while dancing or gymnastics are going on downstairs, and the dreamer may be torn between the two:* ** Intellectual life v. passions. *If the noise of the dancing is drowning the lecture:* ** The intellect is being threatened. *If the voices upstairs are not clearly discernible:* ** The conscious mind is only beginning to understand, is not yet clear.

** The home, and possibly the mother in particular.

Work on the house, cementing, repairing, etc.: ** Work on family relations; attempts to repair emotional rifts. In the same way people may act symbolically in waking life, repairing and redecorating their homes, when it is really the relationship with their partner which is in need of reparation.

Moving to a larger house: * A craving for space or for a more expansive way of life.

A small house especially, or the house where the dreamer was born: * The mother's body, especially the womb; perhaps a regressive fantasy to evade current problems.

** Stable domestic life. Civilization and civilized attitudes. To the rootless nomadic wanderers, when buildings and houses have this particular significance, they appear as a trap and a nightmare. Men are more apt to be restless in this respect than women, and this part of themselves (§ ARCHE-TYPES, the Man's Self) often has to escape the house, for a while at least.

†: *Buildings/waste areas or Construction/demolition:* ** The creative v. the destructive elements in the dreamer.

An impressive, awe-inspiring house: ** The 'house' of the soul, the Self (§ ARCHETYPES).

Balcony (or ledge, sill, etc.) ** The mother's breast. *Especially if accompanied by a feeling of bliss, while leaning on it, enjoying the wonderful view, etc.:* ** A romantic desire to regress to babyhood rather than continue on in life.

Doors ** An opening in the body.

The front door: ** Vagina, female genitalia.

The back door: ** Anus.

Arches: * The pubic arch.

Breaking down the door, especially if the lock is broken and the door can't be closed again: ** Defloration.

Opening and closing the door: ** Intercourse, though the dreamer has a somewhat mechanical attitude to it.

Being too weak to open the door: ** A waning life impulse; being too ill to make love.

** The threshold of the mind and the inner life. Doors to new understanding and awareness.

A door between the outer and inner rooms: ** The way from conscious to unconscious processes.

** Ways in, and therefore the means of being attacked and overpowered, or in any way discovered.

Barring the door: ** A means of self-protection, perhaps unnecessary (§ PEOPLE, the Intruder).

If an animal or person forces his way in, and destroys the lock: ** That particular form of self-protection (possibly childish?) wasn't adequate and is in any case no longer available to the dreamer.

** A way out: a means of escape. *Escaping by another door:* * The dreamer has got the better of the situation (§ ESCAPE).

* A gateway leading towards or away from the individual's redemption, salvation (§ GATES).

Knocking on the door: * 'Knock and ye shall enter'.

Hall ** Vagina.

Lift

Going up and down in the lift: ** A similar action within the body, therefore coitus.

A lift ascending: May be bringing contents from the unconscious up into the conscious mind (§ ASCENDING).

Descending and getting stuck: ** Burial and therefore death.

Passages *These may be dark or get narrower as the dreamer goes along them:* ** Returning to the womb (§), or being born (§ BIRTH; TUNNELS).

Room ** The woman as mother, because both are capable of containing a human being. The womb. And if radiant, the Great Mother (§ ARCHETYPES, a Woman's Self).
A small room with only one door, a basement with water in it: May help to emphasize the fact that the dream is referring to the womb (§).
A series of rooms: * A series of women.
** The chambers of the mind, the psyche, the soul.
Anything in an upstairs room: ** An idea.
The basement or cellar: ** The unconscious.
If the squareness of the room is particularly noticed: * The wholeness of the inner psyche (§ SHAPES, Square).
Leaving the room, going into the next room: * Dying.
Empty rooms: * Empty days (§ Being ENCLOSED).

Stairs
Climbing the stairs: ** A series of rhythmical movements with increasing breathlessness, therefore coitus, which also may be what is likely to take place in the bedroom at the top of the stairs. ** Mounting, ascending, towards the top floor, which may signify the mind (the mystical?). * 'Moving upstairs': promotion.
Going downstairs: Could be to collect provisions or to delve into the unconscious.

Walls
Walls closing in: ** Birth contraction (§ BIRTH).
A brick wall, rampart, or fortress wall, etc.: ** The dark dividing wall between the individual and reality, the apparent impossibility of going on – being 'up against a wall'.

Windows ** Eyes: the 'windows of the soul'. The means by which we look outward, assess reality, etc.
Looking through a window: ** The dreamer's outlook on the world: notice the view, whether bleak, cold and dark, or sunlit and attractive.

Opening a window: ** Giving vent to one's urges, a means of escape to wider horizons, as well as a way of letting in a breath of fresh air, which may consist of outside opinion.

** Female genitalia, especially if the window is on the ground floor front. *Breaking through such a window (or glass door):* ** Defloration.

Stained-glass windows: ** The pattern of the dreamer's life (§ SHAPES). *If illumined by sunlight:* ** The conscious light thrown on it.

Other Buildings, *with particular features that don't apply to buildings in general.* (If the building seems to resemble some other edifice, it may represent that other edifice in the dream: thus a house or courtyard that looks a bit like a church may represent a church in the dream.)

Boarding House ** Marriage, an aspect of which is bed and board.

Castle, Fortress, Citadel ** Woman, but at her most formidable, impregnable. * The 'fortress of knowledge', which may also have to be stormed and plundered.

The courtyard: ** A place of seclusion and safety, often in contrast with a region of danger and fear outside. (If particularly square or circular, § SHAPES.)

Church (including crosses, candlesticks, etc.) ** The appropriate background for ideas about the altruistic moral and religious instinct. The individual's idealism may also be repressed, giving rise to a conflict that may not be acknowledged, but that still expresses itself in dreams. And because of his refusal to face this conflict, the setting may be the only clue as to what the dream is really about.

Desecrating a church (by drinking in it, holding a party there, etc.): * Violating the religious instinct or something else (or someone?) the dreamer ought to respect.

** A place of peace and refuge: possibly the mother ('Mother' Church) or the Self.

* A place of baptism, therefore of rebirth.

City ** The community.

The dreamer's whereabouts in the city and attitude to it: ** His position within the community and relationship with it.

* The Mother Archetype (§); the city harbours its inhabitants like children.

A square in the town or city, especially if the dreamer doesn't know it, so that its abstract shape is more important than any particular associations: * Quaternity, the whole Self (§ SHAPES, Square).

Igloo ** Womb.

Pyramids * Womb (though it certainly must have other associations) (§ SHAPES, Triangle).

Temple ** 'The temple of the soul': the Self (§ ARCHE-TYPES).

Tower (obelisk, steeple, lighthouse, etc.) May be a distorted image of the phallus; may signify male potency that hasn't been consciously acknowledged and that the dreamer has not dared to face – possibly for good reasons? The images may help the dreamer understand the inner creative meaning of these forces.

The tower: * 'A tower of strength': therefore somebody who impresses the dreamer as such: a man of substance, authority. Or, a tower of faith.

The lighthouse: * Warning: saving from the rocks and guiding safely to port. Possibly the church to which the dreamer belonged in his youth.

BULLDOZER (Steamroller, etc.) May be used to knock down barriers, which are often inhibitions, or to crush people, possibly the dreamer himself(?), in which case the machine will represent the crushing person or force.

BURIED ALIVE ** The experience of being born, which

has only registered by the unconscious (§ BIRTH). ** An unwholesome relationship with the mother that is stifling the individual (§ FAMILY). ** Difficulty in breathing; the dream may refer to some illness, tuberculosis for example.

CANNIBALISM

** A way of assimilating the power of the other person, taking possession of his ideas; possibly an image for living off his money. It could also refer to the same symbolism in the Blessed Sacrament: eating and thereby becoming one with Christ.

The most sophisticated cannibals ate only the brains of the other person. The act, entirely ritualistic and symbolic, implied augmenting one's powers with those of another. And what primitive men did still lurks in the recesses of the civilized mind. Wanting to acquire the other person's qualities could indicate envy.

** Devouring passion – 'I could devour him' – possibly with an element of oral sadism.

* Being reincorporated into the parents as we were disgorged from them, and therefore a reversal of the process of birth (§).

Being CARRIED *** The pre-walking stage; may refer to a regressive urge, a desire to make the minimum of effort. Possibly a sinking into autoerotic pleasure – and being 'carried away'; but anyway letting others 'carry' the dreamer, rather than exerting himself.

* The proper acceptance of circumstances that are beyond the individual's control.

If letting himself be carried leads on, in the dream, to danger, disaster, ruin: This will confirm that the first interpretation is more likely to be the correct one.

CASTRATION *** The fear of being emasculated linked

with the desire to be so: a conflict raging between the masculine and feminine (Anima) sides of the individual's personality (§ ARCHETYPES). The individual may be overidentifying with his Anima; or more likely, the conscious mind is dissociating from it completely – instead of knowing and controlling the feminine in him – with the result that the Anima is initially manifesting her desire for recognition in dreams and later may erupt into the individual's life by taking possession of his personality in order to remedy this onesidedness. The dream will more than likely be referring to homosexuality, latent or otherwise.

*** The fear of manhood with its responsibilities: the fear of grappling with real life. But this stems from and is intrinsically linked with the equally strong fear of never growing up, never becoming wholly a man; of being overshadowed and overpowered by others, especially in competition for woman(?), and is related ultimately to fear of impotence in old age. So the dream could refer to a dire loss of energy, which might be the result of too much self-reliance – and Godlessness(?).

CATASTROPHES (explosions, bombs, etc.) ** The demand for a change of attitude (§ EARTHQUAKES; WATER, Floods).

CAVES ** The recess of the mind: the unconscious. The site of mystery and of healing.

Descending into a cave: * A necessary descent from a too exalted conscious position. *Dread of not finding the way out again:* * Fear of lunacy.

** An entrance to the realms of the past which lie buried under the earth and in us. The primitive cave-dweller, to whose instinct for lovemaking we owe our present existence.

** Entrances into the earth: an image of woman, therefore the vagina and the womb, and possibly the mother Archetype (§).

Killing the dragon that guards the cave: May be in order to gain access to the Anima, who will in turn guide the individual to the attainment of wholeness, the treasure of integrity, and so on. More simply, disposing of the father in order to satisfy an incestuous wish with the mother.

* Hermitages, ascetic isolation; a necessary period of incubation in order to prepare for renewal, rebirth.

CEMETERIES ** Thoughts about someone who is dead; or what is dead and buried, namely, the past; and that corner of the mind where old impressions have been buried. There may be something in the past which the dreamer doesn't want to be reminded of or look at too closely.

** A suitable background to evoke the mood of melancholy and depression in which the dreamer's thoughts are plunged.

* The place where the dreamer will meet his God: therefore the dreamer's religious side, as well as his sense of continuity with the past. By presenting a broader view of the sweep of life, the dream may be trying to mitigate a sense of inner confusion.

Being CHASED (pursued or followed) *** Being obsessed, dogged, haunted by something that the dreamer longs to escape or evade; but since the dreamer organizes all parts of the dream, there may be a conflict between what the dreamer is afraid of, yet also longs for.

Being followed by somebody of the opposite sex: ** A love that haunts the dreamer and at least plays a part in his mental life. Or the longing to be wooed, chased after, loved.

Being chased by hostile animals: ** The dreamer is trying to escape his own hostile tendencies or some other aspect of his animal instincts.

The person or thing pursuing the dreamer may represent a fixed idea (§ PEOPLE, as ideas), a reproach, etc., from which the dreamer cannot free himself. And the feeling of persecution may in fact be quite unwarranted.

Somebody else being chased: ** The dreamer's unconscious resentment and aggression towards that person. Or the dreamer may have projected himself on to the pursuer and is thus depicting his own pursuit and therefore love of the person being chased.

CLEAN/Dirty ** Moral conduct.
Dirty clothes, hands, etc.: ** Behaviour the dreamer considers immoral. For example, after losing their virginity, women have sometimes dreamed of wearing a white dress with a stain down the front.

CLIMBING *** Striving towards success, to be above everyone else; may be in sex, ambition, social climbing or ideals.
If the goal is unattainable for some reason (perhaps the road is too steep for the vehicle or the person, or the gravel is loose and the ground gives way): *** The dreamer may be too ambitious – and to no avail – or even too idealistic. If the aim is more modest and doesn't ignore other important, though less altruistic, features of life, the final goal may be reached all the sooner. Or he may just be struggling for a sexual potency that no man possesses.

CLOCKS (watches, other timepieces) * The heart, and therefore the emotions.

CLOTH (fabric, etc.) ** The fabric of life.
The patterns, colours: These may express the nature of the conflict or whatever (§ COLOURS; SHAPES, Patterns).
A square patch of cloth may have the same significance as an abstract square (§ SHAPES, Square).

CLOTHES *** The individual's façade, or persona: his poses, attitudes and role in the world; the thoughts and feelings others expect of him, rather than those that are really his. This façade also serves as a protection against having the skin (and therefore the real self and real feelings) touched; this can be carried too far, and become too permanent.

The dream may reveal the conflict between the person's inner needs and what the world demands of him, or point to the contrast between the performer in his role, and the individual himself.

Being overdressed, possibly in uniform or even armour; being unable to take the clothes off; the garment that grows fast to the skin, the shirt that cannot be torn from the body, etc.: ******* The danger of conforming too much to other people's views instead of developing the character quite independently. In order to be true to himself, the individual assumes his particular part in life merely for convenience, wears and discards it like a costume, never identifying with it.

Being underdressed, wearing rags, underclothes, or dingy or unsuitable clothes (a transparent gown at a reception), including being naked (§): ******* The refusal to play a role, to conform to the way others think of you. This failure to adopt a collective image, or a deliberate rejection of the whole idea, often leads to extreme defensiveness, a spiral of defiance and unsociability; the individual may become unable to relate to others when he wants to.

Clothes being passed on from one person to another: for example, clothes that really belong to the dreamer's mother being worn by his wife in the dream: ****** The new person – the wife in this case – is now playing the same role in the dreamer's life as the former owner-wearer of the clothes. Some earlier experience is being repeated.

A man wearing women's clothes: ****** The dreamer longs to display his feminine side, possibly to the extent of becoming homosexual. His conflict with this tendency may be expressed by his wearing women's clothes on the left side and men's on the right.

A uniform on a woman: May be to make her seem more masculine.

To change clothes: ****** An attempt to change oneself, even if only outwardly.

Wearing trousers that are too short: ****** The wish to be a growing boy again; therefore infantilism.

Clothes that have been cut off short: ***** Other pleasures that have been cut short; pleasures of youth(?).

Pretty clothes: ****** Youth, innocence, boyhood; obviously being brought to an end if they are then dyed black.

Clothes belonging to a particular person: ****** That person. Even some detail of clothing may help reveal the true identity of someone in the dream (§ PEOPLE), especially if the detail of clothing is associated with someone who means a lot to the dreamer (even though the wearer of the clothes is of no particular interest).

The setting or place (§) where the clothes are worn may change their implications drastically. Someone who dreamed of being measured for and trying on an ordinary suit in a church had a frustrated desire to become a priest.

Clothes conceal nudity and therefore sexuality; hence they often have sexual implications. *Underclothes:* ** What is not usually seen, hidden (possibly unconscious?) attitudes to sex. *A tie:* ** Phallus. *Getting undressed:* ** Shedding moral inhibitions.

The colour (§) of the clothing is often significant: *Someone wearing black:* ** An underlying antagonism towards that person: the dreamer may wish him dead. *Wearing a white shirt and black trousers:* May emphasize the contrast between the upper conscious attitudes, which would appear to be pure and enlightened, and the 'shady' instinctual and sexual realms. *Similarly, a white square patch on black clothing:* The conscious approach surrounded by the unconscious.

Coat (and especially cloak) *** Warmth, therefore love.
In a woman's dream: *** The loving protection of a man (father, husband, etc.).
In man's dream, a man in a coat: * A man with a wife, who has seen to it that he is well wrapped before venturing out.
The coat may be too short, not thick enough: ** The inadequacies of the love concerned.
** Protection: often referring to the protection of faith and of God, Who provides covering for the birds and animals, as well as adornment for the lilies. *A sheepskin coat* may emphasize this significance (§ SHEEP).
Fear of losing the coat: * Fear of losing one's faith.

Hat *** The phallus or the vagina, depending on whether the pointed outside or the hollow inside is emphasized (§ OBJECTS, hollow, pointed). A woman's or a man's hat may be a phallic symbol.
Something put into the hat: ** Coitus.
* Halo. *A child in an odd hat:* * Christ.

Raincoat ** Outer protection in general but in particular the membrane enclosing the foetus before birth; a womb fantasy (?).

Shoes *Lacing up shoes:* A well-known symbol of death (Stekel).

Veil (or veil-like garments) ** Something the dreamer will only partially recognize, probably about himself.
If the dreamer is wearing the veil: ** Something about himself that he wishes to keep veiled, or reveal only partially.

CLOUDS ** Vague reveries: 'head in the clouds'; the unreal. Or a hankering for escape and the easy way out. Alternatively, a dim, 'clouded' vision; the clouds come between the individual and the sun, a symbol of the conscious mind.
Clouds laden with rain: * Refreshment for the soil, which may bring on the harvest, and therefore impending growth, fertility or renewal. But also possible devastation and ruin if the rain is too heavy.

COLD *** Emotionally cold, whether hard-hearted or sexually frigid. *Landscapes of ice may have to be traversed, blocks of ice chiselled through, etc., in order to reach someone of the opposite sex.*
* Fear: 'shivering' with fear as well as cold; breaking into a cold sweat.

COLOURS
Drab, dull colours (black, brown, dark) predominating: ** Depression; perhaps thoughts about death.
Bright, colourful dreams: *** Elated states: great vitality in the dreamer.
A change from dull-coloured or black-and-white dreams to highly colourful later dreams: ** The dreamer's improved state of mind; or possibly a process of spiritual growth at work, especially if a bird were to change from black to white to many-coloured.

68

The object coloured will naturally make a difference to the significance of the colour, so the symbolic implications of object and colour must be juggled and jostled until the sense emerges. In the *Bardo Thodol*, for example, there is a progression from coloured animals and figures to coloured images of deities, which then give way to misty colours that in turn are replaced by pure colour, which then vanishes into the primordial Bright Light – all signifying a gradual movement towards transcending the deception of the senses and the ego, in order to know reality.

On the other hand, it may be that the significance of the colours has to be abstracted from the objects, which are merely incidental and can be ignored. The dream may possibly be referring to something entirely different in shape and size, but of the same colours, which the dreamer can discover only through his associations with that colour.

Like the four elements (§ ARCHETYPE, Self), there are also colours closely associated with the four faculties of the mind:

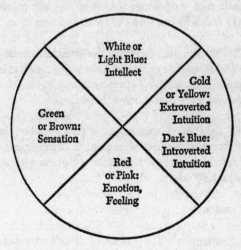

When a combination of these colours appears in a dream – possibly a yellow house, a green tree, blue and red pictures in a book – it is particularly important to be able to abstract them sufficiently to relate them to the functions of the mind. There may be one notable exception (§ MIND, ARCHETYPES).

Black ** The colour of mourning and death. Gloom and depression. ** Anything obscure, dark, secret – especially the contents of the unconscious, including the underworld of hell. ** The dark, earthy, and passive principle of Yin. The feminine and therefore the Mother figure (§ ARCHETYPES), whose principal colours are black or red.

Blue ** The celestial, the heavenly and therefore spiritual energy. Also the intellect; intellectual understanding; cool, mature reasoning. Blue has also been associated with fidelity.
A dark blue that would be associated more with water and the depths of the sea than with the sky: ** Introverted intuition. An intuitive understanding of inner realities, such as archetypes (§) and patterns of the soul rather than other people. (Contrast with Yellow, below.)
Deep blue mixed with green: * Liberation. The freedom of the sea(?) or a union of opposites: sensation and intuition(?).

Brown ** Excrement (§ BODY), which in turn has often been associated with gold or money. It is also the colour of the earth (§) and is linked with the faculty of sensation.

Gold ** The sun, and therefore the conscious mind and the truth. The masculine principle. Like yellow, gold may signify intuition.
†: *Gold/silver:* ** Masculine v. feminine.

Green ** Everything that grows; vigour, vitality, life itself. Hope: the green pastures of heaven(?). Being 'green' implies inexperience, simplicity; also jealousy ('green with envy'); or simply looking seasick, ill.

Lilac * Death.

Orange (Saffron) * The colour of Buddhist robes. Occult power.

Pink (Rose) ** The emotions. Something pleasant but illusory: a 'rosy' outlook, the 'rose-coloured glasses' of love.
If specifically rose: * Somebody named Rose.

Purple * Vital power.

Red ** Blood, fire, wine. Therefore the emotions as well as sexual excitement; also anger: 'seeing red', getting red-faced with anger.
Especially red tunnels, corridors: ** Menstruation.

White (Silver) ** Light: the pure light of illumination, self-knowledge, wisdom; the Divine mind. Innocence, purity.
Soiled white: ** Defloration.
†: *White/Black, especially one white and one black animal:* *** The light, innocent side of one's nature v. the dark, shadowy side. *Especially if silver or round:* ** The moon (§) the light in the dark, therefore in the unconscious. Also the feminine.
White liquid, such as milk: ** Semen.
   Externally, in the outside world in contrast with the inner world, white is the colour of many creatures or plants unaccustomed to the light (grass under a stone, for example).

Yellow ** Extroverted intuition, that is, oriented towards the external object, the other person. Or cowardice.
Yellow liquid: ** Urine (§ BODY).
Dull yellow: * Death.

CONFLICT Even when a series of dreams isn't specifically about struggles and battles, wrestling matches, hunts, dreadful decisions or obvious contrasts between opposites, it will be impossible to understand the dreams properly without relating them to the individual's current problems and general conflicts. Because dreams compensate for inadequate or bigoted conscious attitudes, the conflict often expresses itself in the many contrasts between the individual's dream life and his waking life.
   The mind is an arena in which many different forces are struggling for mastery, and this inner turmoil is continually reflected and refracted in dreams. 'The dreamer's life conflict finds expression in every dream.'
   If one aspect of the inner conflict is being deliberately ignored,

the unconscious tension and anguish that result are often unbearable and extremely damaging to the personality. The character thrives on an open struggle, but this hidden tension only exhausts and wears it out, and is far more likely to be the cause of a nervous breakdown, for example, than any merely external hardship or difficulty (apart from leading to further hardships and difficulties). Dreams frequently reveal the factors that are being ignored, and in increasingly striking images.

Resolving the conflict. The dream may indicate how the inner life can be adapted to the circumstances, or how the circumstances themselves may be changed or modified. But most often it is necessary to face the conflict, which is often just a personal share in the general struggle in nature between life and death, with the utmost courage and strength, and a determination not to evade either side of the issue. For example, if a series of dreams reveal that a person's instincts are being stifled by his moral code, there is no advantage in stifling his morality instead.

This approach to the conflict brings the individual into contact with his inner forces, which are often the source of considerable energy; it also stimulates greater efforts and opens up new possibilities. The greater the problem, the greater the possibility of growth. And even when a particular problem is solved, it usually leads to another. Without conflict there is often only stagnation or, worse still, a pseudo-problem, a feeble substitute worry, which is trumped up in order to evade tackling the real issues of life.

CONFUSING (one object for another) ** Inner mental confusion.

COOKING ** Transforming the raw material into something more digestible, possibly some truth – about himself? – that the dreamer finds hard to swallow; or whatever is being cooked may refer to something in the dreamer that he is trying to change.

Turning something over in the pan: ** Turning it over in the mind.

Round pan: * A circle (§ SHAPES).
** Home life; †: Domesticity v. wider horizons; the hunger for experience.

COUNTING * 'Counting on', depending or relying on.

COVER ** 'Cover up', lie, hide, deceive.

CRAWLING *** Memories of childhood, perhaps accompanied by the desire to return to it. Or the child in the dreamer who wants recognition of his needs. †: The longing to regress to childhood v. the moving on into adulthood and its responsibilities.
Crawling into tunnels, etc.: ** Being born (§ BIRTH).
Someone else crawling: * The wish to put that person down, 'make him crawl'.

CRIMES Crime is the best visual image of high degrees of emotion.
To kill: ** Extreme hate.
To steal: ** Extreme desire. But the image also implies that the dreamer considers himself guilty.
The enormity of a crime may relate to a comparatively trivial incident in life: The dream nevertheless reveals the individual's profound disapproval of his own impulses. Or the dream may refer back to some criminal wish that the conscious mind has rejected, such as wanting the death of a parent. Alternatively, the crime in the dream may point to a quite different crime that the dreamer actually committed. If the crime cannot be related to anything in the past, however, it may be expressing fear (what if that were to happen?) and could account for a feeling of anxiety and withdrawal.
The unconscious may add punishment (§) *to atone for the guilt.*
A criminal figure who has to be restrained may signify the same impulse that appears in other dreams as an animal.
Someone else committing a crime against the dreamer: * Some-

one else is threatening some aspect of the dreamer's life; or one part of himself is stifling another to such an extent that it could be considered criminal.

CROSSING *** An important decision; overcoming obstacles. A decisive step, possibly from childhood to maturity. Or that turning point in the middle of life when the individual's values are undergoing drastic changes. Or the crossing from life to death.

The far bank or the far shore often appears in dreams as the glowing goal, while this shore may be unattainable for one reason or another. The eternal Youth, the Wise Old Man, and especially the Hero (§ ARCHETYPES) may accompany this phase of dreams; in a woman's dreams it will be her Animus. The crossing may be accomplished by ford or bridge, by boat, swimming, or wading, or even by being carried (§) across (but this is ominous).

After the ground of subjective, egocentric existence has been shattered, the Self plunges through despair to find another shore, another destination, or it perishes in the search. What lies behind should relate to the past, what lies ahead to the possible future: the far bank or shore is always the goal; on whether it is reached or not depends the likelihood of success or failure, which may as yet be undecided in the dreamer's mind.

Alligators in the river, etc.: ** Considerable difficulties to be overcome.

At the approach of death people often have especially vivid dreams of crossing fords, gullies, and so on. The dream may indicate how to negotiate this final crossing successfully.

CROWN * Being 'crowned' with success, or the crown of wisdom. Kingly totality, unity, wholeness (§ ARCHETYPES, the Self).

DANCING Is a preliminary to making love, with people and animals alike. ** Making love.

The DARK

Especially a dark nocturnal atmosphere in dreams: ** The dream is dealing with the realm of the unconscious soul, the feminine yielding principle in contrast with the active spirit.

The more dark and menacing the dreams: * The conscious intellect is too self-reliant and is ignoring the emotional passive realm of womanhood. Irrational fear of the dark may be fear that the conscious spirit will be swallowed up again in the aboriginal unconscious from which it emerged by a long process of evolution.

** The unknown in general, or death. Or something that the dreamer doesn't want to look at too clearly; something in the darkened place he would rather not see.

Being cramped in a dark space: ** Being back in the womb (§ BIRTH). ** Gloom, depression (§ PLACE; setting may indicate mood).

DEATH

Someone the dreamer loves dying: Since the dreamer's own unconscious has arranged for the death (§ ACTION), it expresses the hostile, aggressive side of his emotional involvement which finds no outlet in everyday life. Sometimes the death wish may date from childhood, but in any case dreams re-establish the spontaneous attitudes of childhood, which flare up easily. This underlying hostility accompanies almost all cases of intense devotion.

Dreaming of the death of a parent: The ingredient of antagonism in the love is heightened by the son's rivalry for the attention of his mother or the daughter's wanting her mother out of the way in order to be closer to her father. In this case dreams act as a safety valve.

If the dream is accompanied by anxiety: The anxiety may be more about the dreamer's own hostility and aggression than genuinely for the other person. However, there may be an element of wanting a really vivid picture of the other person's death or absence, in order to be able to appreciate him or her all the more on waking.

** A murderous hostility towards the other person whom one genuinely wants out of the way, especially after being jilted, after the breakup of a friendship, etc. Then the dream expresses the desire to forget about that person, relegate him to oblivion. It might be advisable to keep one's distance.

The ground strewn with dead bodies: * The desire to eliminate rivals.

Dreaming of oneself as dead: ** Fear of life and retreat from it. As in many other instances, nobody has improved on the interpretation of Artemidorus or on the way he puts it: 'To dream of death is good for those in fear, for the dead have no more fears.'

It has much the same significance as returning to the womb and may result from a feeling of incompetence, helplessness, disorientation, estrangement, which may in turn be the result of ignoring, repressing, rejecting too much of oneself: feeling too responsible for the way one is made.

Similarly, in waking life a suicidal impulse means a desire to retreat from the demands of life; Freud thought that fear of heights or open spaces indicated a suicidal impulse to which the body responded with trembling, fits, etc.

** The old self dying: The death of egotism and self-centredness. *Lying in a coffin:* * Death of the old personality in order to make way for the birth of the new; liberation.

If rigor mortis has set in: ** A constricted, pressurized, fearful and therefore rigid mental outlook (§ STIFF).

The appearance of Death or of someone who is actually dead: ** The dreamer can no longer afford to ignore the fact of his own death. *If the figure stares the dreamer in the face:* ** Death stares him in the face, though he's been refusing to acknowledge it.

* Frigidity, impotence.

The death, however, may have other, quite personal associations: for example, a woman dreamed of the death of yet another relative only in order to see the man she loved at the funeral again. Or the dreamer may have dreamt a death solely in order to attract the sympathy that a bereavement would afford him.

DEEP ** The profound.
Deep water, deep caves: ** The further recesses of the mind, where something may have been repressed(?). The devouring aspect of the Mother Figure (§ ARCHETYPES) which threatens to swallow one up(?).
Unplumbed depths: * Womanhood.

DESCENDING ** Weakening, degenerating.
Descending into the earth, a cave, an abyss: ** A necessary descent into the underworld, the unconscious, in order to retrieve and bring to light certain aspects of one's personality. Also, death.

DESERT ** Isolation, loneliness, or an arid emptiness and desolation within. A lost paradise.

DRAMA (film, play, television show) Such performances in a dream usually depict the drama of the individual's own life, and usually some unpleasant aspect of it with which he doesn't want to be associated, so he surveys it from a distance – that is, loses himself in the audience. There may be an element of looking at one's problems objectively, from a spectator's point of view.
The theatre: ** The mind – 'the theatre of the mind' – and the action of the play: what is going on in it. The dream will be an act of introspection.

If the dreamer taking part in the play suddenly doesn't know his lines and has to improvise : May be demanding of the individual a more spontaneous attitude to life; he should meet its challenges by improvising freely, creatively, rather than being parrot-like and rigid in his responses or trying to anticipate and prepare for every event.
The prompter : * Promptings from the unconscious.

The DREAM WITHIN A DREAM The dreamer is trying to persuade himself that something unsavoury is only a dream. What would otherwise seem all too real and meaningful is devalued, reduced to a fantasy and need not be reckoned with. This is a way of dismissing what the mind is trying to communicate, or perhaps the other way round: the mind may know only too well that the one way to get the individual to recognize unpalatable facts is by making them appear harmless.

DRINK * The earliest form of nourishment, hence drinking may be hinting at a tendency or a desire to return to babyhood (especially if drunk from the mouth of the bottle).

Alcohol Dissolves inhibitions, which may release sexual appetites. ** Excitement, intoxication, ecstasy. People also drink to feel younger and more lively. ** Rejuvenation; the water of life; a return to a younger period of life.
Red wine : * Blood. *Spilling red wine :* * Spilling blood, killing.
Spirits : * The spirit.

Milk * Semen. Men apparently require a greater proportion than women of liquid nourishment, while women's intake of solid food is larger.

EARTH *The whole earth or any part of it; its cities as well as its country; the land with its woods, and also the sea:* ******* Matter itself; the realm of the feminine – 'Mother Earth' – and the Great Mother (§ ARCHETYPES).

The land evokes lasting firmness, the passive principle, the warmth and peace of the family, and is a more familiar and friendly image than the sea (§ WATER). It is hostile only in extremes: for example, volcanoes, earthquakes, crags.

Underground: ****** The lower regions of the soul; the hidden and infernal realms. Everyone who wishes for rebirth in some less ephemeral form than the ego must first pass through this underworld where the ego dies. Also, the realm of the dead and of the past.

Earthquakes ****** Disruption. Old attitudes crumbling. The world of our certainties, habits and beliefs falling apart. The 'ground' of the mind is being prepared for great changes. The dreamer is probably beginning to shift the egotistical focus of his attention to a more objective view of himself, life and reality. The Shadow often appears in dreams of this type (§ ARCHETYPES).

Mud ****** The primeval swamps from which we came, therefore the womb (§). If the dream isn't about retreating from difficulties into the womb, it may be the opposite: escape from an overprotective situation that is stifling the dreamer. ****** Excrement (§ BODY). Healing: mud baths.

Sinking into a bog or quagmire: ****** Death. May also be a sexual image, especially if limbs are pulled in and out of the mud, and will reveal that the dreamer's unconscious regards sex as dirty.

**Volcanoes ** ** Subterranean forces, that is, repressed passions and impulses erupting to the surface.

**EATING ** ** Assimilating the strength of what is eaten, the symbolic significance of which may have to be discerned. (§ CANNIBALISM, for eating a person.)
** Participation with the other figures present: if they are ARCHETYPES, it will indicate an integration of the personality; if they are actual people, some very close link with them could be implied, often marriage.

However, eating something is also a primitive way of destroying it; this will be a likely interpretation if there is an element of tearing it apart with one's teeth like an animal.

Banquet * Pleasures of the flesh (§ APPETITES).

Being Eaten (swallowed, devoured) The jaws of death, which may be symbolic of the extinction of consciousness and the death of the ego. Rescue is imperative, for both the ego and consciousness have their essential functions; but where some hope of escape is indicated, this period in the bowels of some monster, monstrous fish, etc.: ** A temporary period of gestation; maturing in the dark. The conscious ego is being mortified and purged, but only so that it can penetrate more deeply into the nature of reality and everything outside itself. *Being devoured in the West, where the sun sets, is especially likely to lead to the rebirth (sunset is followed by sunrise).*

EGG * *** Potential life, which must first be fertilized from the outside; dark matter that must be penetrated by the light of consciousness before it can come to fruition in the birth of new being. ** The Self (§ ARCHETYPES). (In alchemy the inner complete and perfect man emerges from an egg.)
** Easter and the Resurrection, which confirms the symbolism, except that Christ is the Light which penetrates matter and emerges from the tomb reborn.

EMOTIONS The emotion that accompanies each dream is sometimes exaggerated a bit, but is rarely distorted in any other way. It therefore often provides a vital clue to the otherwise unrecognizable contents of a dream.

Emotions are considered to be the chief contents of the personal unconscious, just as the three chief archetypes are the main contents of the collective unconscious. Emotions and archetypes are thought to be the original source of all dreams.

From the emotional standpoint, taking dreams as pictorial representations of the dreamer's emotional life, the unconscious images become considerably more coherent than the other way round, which makes it hard to explain why trivial dream-scenes should often be accompanied by intense and totally inappropriate emotions. So the anxiety, fear, shame or panic, as well as the pride, joy, desire and love that accompany the dream, must be fastened on to and related to the dreamer's waking life. In this way the real underlying subject matter of the dream may be disclosed: for example, if the dream is accompanied by anxiety, it will relate to something the individual is anxious about, and possibly to similar past anxieties.

Anger § AGGRESSION.

Anxiety (Fear) A dream accompanied by anxiety will probably refer to whatever the individual is most anxious about at the time: if he is chiefly concerned about his career, it is probably about that; if he is more worried about a personal relationship, that is likely to be the subject of the dream, whatever its superficial form.

A lot of anxiety arises from the discrepancy between the individual's actual life and the way he feels it should be lived. Fear accompanies being separated from one's essential needs: when longing is no longer enough to urge a man to achieve his desire, then fear prods him from behind. By accepting fear as a part of nature, at least the individual isn't afraid of fear. On the other hand, the fear may be a hangover from a situation that is no longer relevant, in which case the dream could be trying to get the dreamer to realize and dismiss it consciously, rather than leave it lurking vaguely in the unconscious, where it still has power to cloud his outlook.

The dream that superficially gratifies an infantile wish, yet is accompanied by terror, may be pointing out the danger of indulging this wish – the threat to the personality.

Desire This may be instinctual and compulsive, or considered and controlled. The more the individual seeks to understand and direct his desires, the less likely they are to erupt in a devastating way, first in his dreams and then in life. Any symbol that expresses an equivalent intensity of desire may be used, regardless of any other considerations; hence, a moth flying into a naked flame can be an image of a man's desire for God.

Indifference *A scene that should arouse the dreamer's emotions but leaves him cold in the dream:* could be trying to draw attention to his lack of feeling, his neglect of the emotional side of his life (§ MIND, ARCHETYPES).

Wonder Somebody who has eradicated all feeling from his waking life may suddenly be amazed and filled with wonder in his dreams to see what he thought didn't exist: when conscious control is relaxed by sleep, other provinces of the mind may assert themselves. The dream may thus try to illustrate that the individual can't be attuned to the whole of reality as long as half his mind is shut down.

This inspiring quality usually accompanies archetypal dreams. Whatever the image, if it is radiant, divinely impressive, godlike, mysterious, it will probably relate to the archetypes (§).

Being ENCLOSED (Confined, etc.) ** The barricades between the individual and the outside world: the dream may relate to the original experience of being born – emerging from a confined space to encounter life – but it will also refer to the present situation: if the individual can pin down what aspect of himself feels confined, needs more scope, and what it is that is hemming him in – possibly the home, the family circle, a destructive parent – then the images will probably convey the rest vividly enough.

What was initially a useful means of protection often turns into a deathtrap, if there is no way in or out. The defences against the outside world may be so strong and impregnable that the individual's whole life is devoid of emotional content. What seemed stable is really stagnant and seething within. It is the inner that breaks up if it can't be penetrated from outside. In contrast with finding an inner sanctuary (§ BUILDINGS, Courtyard), the individual needs greater contact with the outside world.

Opening a door with difficulty or just a shift in the action from an enclosed place to the outer world in later dreams: will probably mark a significant improvement in the individual's situation.

Figures trapped in a glass sphere, a transparent bubble, or a flask of any kind: * Some aspect of the dreamer that wants to be realized, be born.

ENTWINING, Entangling *A serpent, an octopus, a creeper on a tree, etc.:* ** Emotional 'entanglements' from which the dreamer wishes to extricate himself – often with the possessive mother (§ FAMILY; ARCHETYPES, the Terrible Mother).

ESCAPE

Something that escapes from the dreamer: ** Something that has 'escaped' his mind or slipped his memory, or which he has failed to grasp.

When one way is blocked, finding another way out: ** The dreamer has managed to evade whatever threatened him; he has got the better of the situation, as the image makes plain. This could mark the end of a series of dreams, a particular conflict having been concluded successfully, or it may just indicate a temporary respite from that theme.

EXAMS ** Concern about some new test in life, often the wedding night. The dreamer's self-confidence may be at stake. Or an impending decision, probably about him, rather than by him.

If the dreamer is unprepared and unsuccessful in the dream, he may nevertheless be trying to reassure himself that everything will turn out all right, especially if he is going through an exam that he actually passed in life.

* The ultimate test: his conscience may be apprehensive about how his whole life will be judged, in which case the dream may reveal an unacknowledged religious tendency and fear of the wrath of God.

EXCHANGING (one object or person for another) ** A proposed change in the dreamer.

Exchanging a male prisoner for a female prisoner: * A change from homosexuality to heterosexuality.

Having too many trousers and not enough jackets, and swapping the trousers for some jackets to make suits: ** Too great an emphasis on the lower instinctual realm which is now being changed, put right.

FAILURE The dream may indicate whether the goal is actually unattainable, and therefore the aim in life to which it refers should be abandoned altogether, or if it is being approached in the wrong way, but could eventually be successful if it were tackled differently.

FALLING ** Insecurity, which is inevitably accompanied by anxiety, and may be a genuine insight into the failure and misfortune looming ahead. (§ EMOTIONS, Anxiety (Fears).) 'Being dropped, even into bed, is terror itself – the first definite form of insecurity, even of death. All our lives we speak of misfortune as a "fall"; we fall into the enemy's hands, fall from grace, fall upon hard times' (Langer).

If the dream refers to falling into temptation, the dislike of falling will signify disapproval, the other side of the inner conflict.

The dream may relate to the fall 'from the uterine heaven to the terrestrial abyss' (Fodor; § BIRTH), and so refer to the Fall of Man.

In a woman's dream : ** Yielding, therefore sexual intercourse; 'the essential feature of female sexuality – the falling and sinking' (Schwarz).

The landing : * Coitus, the earth being a symbol of womanhood. The soft or hard landing being the relative damage the dreamer is doing himself: for example, if the landing is softer than he expected, he may be hoping that in spite of his anxieties about this particular relationship, it may in fact not work out so badly.

Other people falling : * Unconscious death wishes (§ DEATH).

Or a man may dream of a 'fallen' woman, and therefore available without too much responsibility attached.

Climbing and falling: ** Exaggerated ambition is often put up like a barrier against childhood fears, but at times the old fear breaks through again (§ CLIMBING).

* Falling asleep, loss of consciousness, loss of ego. Sleep and death are always associated.

†: The firm v. the yielding; the active v. the passive; awareness and life v. sleep and death.

The Abyss ** The abyss of inner loneliness and despair, or of death. The underlying void, the nothingness from which all was made and therefore the source of all life. Or the open, the receptive, the feminine principle (§ ARCHETYPES, the Great Mother).

Being forced into the abyss: * The need to go down into the unconscious and abandon a too-exalted conscious position; to stoop low and plumb the mysterious depths of life. Concentrating only on the spiritual or the intellectual, to the exclusion of so much else, can also be a limitation.

FAMILY The childhood relationships with the family influence the basic pattern from which all future relationships develop. Because of the intense involvement with the family, its various members may be represented by images and symbols, but rarely the other way round. If a member of the family appears in a dream, he almost certainly represents himself, or the corresponding archetype he has helped to form (that is, the image of fatherhood, motherhood, etc.) within the dreamer.

The loves, the rivalries and the struggles for individuality and independence which take place first within the family, and later in the wider context of life, feature in many dreams, which are often distorted to make the dreamer's own thoughts and conflicts less disconcerting for him.

The Triangle. The basic pattern of relationships within the family is triangular, involving the mother, the father and the child: a love for the parent of the opposite sex and rivalry with the parent of the same sex, often mixed with considerable hostility. This emotional pattern continues throughout life and is reflected in dreams. The most extreme example is when somebody is attracted only by a person already married in order to separate the couple and have one member of it for himself; this is a symbolical re-enactment of the drama of his childhood with a pseudosatisfactory outcome, and is, needless to say, a situation fraught with anxiety.

Love and transferring that love outside the family. The intense loves, and desire for love, often express themselves in dreams as incestuous relationships (§ SEX). Later transferral of this love between mother and son, father and daughter, or brother and sister on to a boyfriend or girlfriend is often difficult, and the difficulties will feature in dreams; if the situation is consciously realized and understood, it can only help. *If the dreamer is enjoying himself with a boyfriend or girlfriend, and is perhaps getting sexually excited, when a member of his family (or image of that person) interrupts or interferes in some way:* ** The dreamer is still emotionally involved with that family member who is interfering with his new relationship, preventing it from going as smoothly as it would otherwise. If the family member crops up (that is, springs to mind) at the moment when the dreamer is getting sexually excited, it may mean that the new sex partner has been confused in the dreamer's mind with the forbidden incestuous relationship, and so is also unconsciously forbidden. In this case the defences and inhibitions, which are no longer required, will gradually have to be torn down.

Any member of the family who appears frequently in dreams; or, equally, someone who never appears and so is remarkable for his absence (§ NEGATIVES); *or occasionally the whole family together, assembled so that picking out one particular person is avoided* (§ PEOPLE, *Crowds*): ** A continued love for that person. (And to avoid the incestuous implications, the dreamer could be encouraging his homosexual tendencies.)

The struggle for individuality. The child's feeling of being crushed or thwarted by his parents often adds to the antagonism of his rivalries – so much so that not many children have gone through childhood without wishing one of their parents dead at one time or another (§ DEATH).

The dreamer rebelling against his parents; or his parents dying or being killed (§ DEATH). ****** The time has come for the child to break away from his parents and take on his own responsibilities and decisions. Thus, getting rid of the parent is simply a vividly pictorial image of shedding his own attachment and dependence.

†: Wanting to grow up and break away from family ties v. apprehension about loss of security and the hazards of the world, often combined with feeling guilty about deserting the parents.

Dreams may depict in various other ways this legitimate necessity for establishing one's independence, so that at a later stage a new relationship can arise, based on mutual affection; the dream will discourage this if the revolt is premature or, possibly, if the rebelliousness has gone on too long.

Discrediting the parent; the father behaving in a drunken or otherwise irresponsible way (quite unlike him in life): ****** The dreamer is hopelessly dependent on his father as a result of too much admiration and respect, and the dream is trying to correct this. The unconscious is illustrating the fact that there is no need to feel inferior – he isn't so perfect. Even though the father may in fact be an exemplary character, he has ceased to be perfect for the dreamer, and is in fact being destructive. From dreams we can find out only a personal image or idea of our family, not what the family is really like. But this idea of them often matters more to the individual than the facts do. The childhood image of the parents is also exaggerated, but this image of them is eventually shattered – an event which continues to crop up in dreams long afterwards (a tarnished object or a shattered image may refer to it).

Killing a parent: ****** The most drastic expression of the need for independence; it may indicate either the immense difficulties of attaining it or that a certain mixture of irrational hidden rage, possibly the result of repressed incestuous longing for one or other of the parents, is involved in the rebelliousness.

Rivalry between two brothers or two sisters: This is nearly always founded on the fear of being rejected by one of the parents in favour of the other brother or sister; it is a manifestation of this underlying insecurity, prolonged even though the situation is no longer relevant (the parent may even be dead). *An older brother:* ***** Somebody else who is at present a powerful opponent.

The family as archetypes and images. Just as the dreamer's first impressions of the father and the mother contribute to the outward forms of the archetypes – his particular image of fatherhood and motherhood – so the actual father and mother may continue to be symbols of these various forces and tendencies in the mind. For example, the parents give life but they also inhibit the child's instincts in order to make him socially acceptable. Thus the actual father may become in dreams more a symbol of the conscious masculine principle, as well as authority and conscience, but also of oppression in his negative aspect; and the mother the symbol of motherhood, nurturing and protecting, but also destructive when over-possessive (§ ARCHETYPES, the Mother/Terrible Mother, the Father/Ogre).

Often this approach to family problems, seeing family members as archetypal figures within human nature, lessens the tension of the situation and lends more significance to the struggle of making the relationships work. For example: *A man shouting at his mother in a dream:* May be seen as doing violence to the feminine principle in himself – the realm of nature and the unconscious. It might be better to listen to what his Anima has to say. If he lets the feminine in his nature respond, it may then come to his aid in solving the problems of the actual relationship. (Once the conscious attitude is altered it usually doesn't take long for the change to be registered in later dreams.)

A man's mother being transformed into his sister, or wife, mistress: * His Anima (§ ARCHETYPES).

Equally, a woman's lover, brother or father, especially if one is transformed into another: * Her Animus.

A man's brother; a woman's sister: * The Shadow (§ ARCHETYPES). There is a typical pattern of strife between brothers which goes back to Cain and Abel. Each will represent the other's Shadow in the inner conflict. But the reconciliation between the two frequently leads to the transformation of both for the better. (If the dreamer doesn't have a brother, the theme of two brothers is all the more likely to point to the moral conflict between good and evil, not confused by any personal associations.)

From this it can be seen that the family circle provides the original pattern of wholeness, which is yet to be cultivated within the individual. His early dependence on three external relationships establishes his first contact with the various archetypal forces at work in nature and the unconscious.

At this unconscious level an astonishing interdependence between various members of the family has been discovered: for example, in *The Lady of the Hare*, Layard describes the remarkable improvement he saw in the daughter while he was working on the mother's dreams; and there are other instances in which what is bottled up in the parents' unconsciouses appears to be lived out by their children. It could well be that brothers or sisters often complement each other in the same way.

Until the individual breaks away from his parents and his family, however, he can never experience the full force of the archetypes as they really are, that is, within his own psyche. The most intimate and profound knowledge of the forces at work in nature can be acquired only by opening up the full range of his own inner being: there is no alternative way of knowing except by using to their utmost capacity the faculties designed for that purpose.

†: Almost all the conflicts and problems of life are experienced first within the family and continue to be reflected in dreams about the family.

FENCES ** Man-made structures imposed over wild nature; therefore inhibitions. Also self-control, especially if they are to hem in wild animals (§ OBSTACLES).

FIELDS * 'Field' of art, or of science, or any learning.
Green fields: ** Green pastures, therefore a spiritual or rightful goal. They sometimes lie on the far bank (§ CROSSING).
Ploughed field: § PLOUGHING.

FIGHTING ** A moral struggle or a mental conflict. (§ CONFLICT; AGGRESSION).

FIRE ******* The warmth of the emotions, but especially passion and desire. (Langer uses fire to illustrate the fact that the symbolic meaning of a thing may be the opposite of its actual nature: 'Fire is a natural symbol of life and passion, though it is the one element in which nothing can actually live.') Symbolically, fire is very much associated with the mouth: both 'lick' and 'devour'; we speak of 'tongues' of fire and 'fiery' words. As with all dream images the obvious associations must be explored first: in the case of an actual fire, for instance a will being burned, hopes are being 'burned'.

A fireplace, hearth, grate: ****** The home.

Rubbing sticks together to make fire: ****** Intercourse.

A building on fire, a forest fire, any fire that is out of control: A fatal outburst of emotion. Extreme uncontrollable passions, their destructive threatening aspect, and perhaps the individual's powerlessness and terror.

†: Fire and water are mutually exclusive and may be used to represent an inner conflict.

Fighting a fire: ****** Calming the passions. (Underlying sexual motives are frequently behind pyromania.)

* Other forms of excitement besides lust: an inner mood of energy, lightness, movement, grace, gaiety. The quick, the adventurous. There may be an element of surprise involved.

* The purging, purifying and transforming quality of fire.

Setting fire to a wheel: ***** A catastrophic revolt against one's destiny, the wheel of fate.

Hellfire: ****** The lower regions of the mind, into which the dreamer must not be too timid to descend for certain vital knowledge before being reborn; this theme runs parallel to Christ's descent into hell before his resurrection.

The end of the world by fire: ****** The end of a particular outlook on the world, possibly leading to a vastly broader view of life, no longer seen from the limited egocentric standpoint.

Flame

When the emphasis is more on the light shed than on the fire's heat or consuming quality: ****** The enlightened spirit, as when the tongues of fire descended at Pentecost. The inner spirit: the Self. Love: 'his flame'.

A candle flame being snuffed out : ** The loss of egoconsciousness.

FISH ** The contents of the deeper layers of the unconscious mind (§ WATER). As one of the primitive ancestors in the scale of evolution it refers to the remote past and comes from a profoundly alien underworld. The saving power of renewal and rebirth may be symbolized by fish, which are often the equivalent of the treasure (§) in the depths of a cave or well.
If the fish has some spiritual quality about it : * The Self (§ ARCHETYPES).
** Coldness, impotence (fish are phallic in shape but cold-blooded). People who are referred to as 'a poor fish' or 'an odd fish' or 'a fish out of water' often have some inability to relate, possibly because of a lack of sexual attractiveness or emotional warmth.
†: *Fish swimming in opposite directions:* * The personal unconscious and the emotions v. the collective unconscious. Such a conflict can be resolved only by adapting the personal whims and feelings to the archetypal pattern.
Fish's eyes: * Perpetual attention, because they never shut.
Fishing: ** Keeping the conscious mind firmly anchored to tangible reality, while trying to catch the treasures of the unconscious. *A big fish may be landed, but if it is too big, the fisherman may become the victim of his catch. Fishing from a boat is plainly more precarious.*
Eating fish: ** Renewal, rebirth: fish is a miraculous food.
Being eaten by a fish: ** Being swallowed by the unconscious. *To be cast up on the shore again:* ** To regain conscious control (but this is the exception).
†: Conscious v. unconscious.

Jellyfish * Whatever makes the individual squirm, especially if it is associated with the sea – the unconscious feminine realm.

Octopus ** The clinging possessive mother (§ ARCHETYPES, the Terrible Mother).

Shellfish ** Female genitalia, because of their shape.

An oyster (etc.) without its shell: ** A lack of persona, façade, with which to confront the hazards of the world (§ CLOTHES, Underdressed).

Crab: * Renewal, because a crab renews its shell. Also, bad luck, 'being crabbed'. (In astrology Cancer, the Crab, is the house of the moon, and its month begins at the time of the summer solstice, when the days begin to get shorter).

Lobster: ** Male genitalia, because of shape and redness.

Whale ** The realm of the feminine, whether the unconscious or the mother.

Being swallowed by the whale: * The story of Jonah, and a dark period in the bowels of nature during which the individual is replenished from the store of the unconscious, to be born anew. (In *Moby Dick* the whale was a symbol of Captain Ahab's Self (§ ARCHETYPES), but because his ego dictated the terms the Self had become negative and destructive.)

FLOWERS ** Vitality, beauty; the blossoming of the individual, often through some new relationship involving love and tenderness. Or: ** The male or female genitalia, depending on the shape (whether pointed or hollow).

Crushed flowers: ** Defloration, loss of virginity.

Blue flowers: ** The flower of the soul, the mystical, the romantic or lyrical. The colour of the flowers may be significant (§ COLOURS).

Circular flowers: * The circle, the mandala (§ SHAPES), or the maternal womb.

Dried flowers: ** Preserving one's love and sex for inspection rather than living it.

Giving flowers, especially if they are dying or dead: * Antagonism, a concealed death-wish towards that person, especially if the most likely time to give flowers to that particular person would be at his funeral. It may also signify the flower-giver's life blossoming through the recipient.

In a man's dream: * The qualities of fantasy and feeling associated with the feminine side of his nature, his Anima.

Clover * Three leaves in one, therefore the Trinity (§ NUM-BERS, Three).

Lily ** Innocence; an incorruptible nature.
The red lily: * The masculine realm.
The white lily: * The feminine realm.

Rose ** Feminine beauty. It is 'harder to associate roses with vegetables than with girls' (Langer). As for the circular flower above: * The circle (§ SHAPES); or the maternal womb.
A rosebud: * A virgin.
Especially with four petals: * The Western equivalent of the Lotus, the mystic rose, the rose of the Rosicrucians, the obvious mandala of the rose-window.

FLYING *** The wish to escape the pull of the earth. 'Flight' from humdrum everyday earthly existence, with all its tedious responsibilities, and therefore often 'flight' into the realms of daydreams and fantasies: 'flights' of fancy and of the mind. *But skimming over the surface of the earth, moving in bounds and hops:* * Keeping an eye on reality, never completely losing contact.
If the dreamer is away a long time, flies off into space or is unable to land again: * The wish to escape the turmoil below may lead to a total lack of realism and even possibly the danger of madness, somebody whose 'feet are off the ground'.
** The desire for freedom may have a more spiritual founda-tion: soaring towards the celestial, the heavenly; the longing for immortality.
** On the practical level the dreamer may wish to transcend and overcome difficulties, to lift himself above the complicated ruts and patterns of life, or to elevate himself above other people, to excel or even to dominate; or just attempt to compensate for a feeling of inferiority. 'To fly is to be lifted above those about one' (Artemidorus).
** On the physical plane, the ecstasy of sensuality: erection and coitus; possibly the desire for free love. Feeling light as air; this could have something to do with recapturing the pleasures of the swing in childhood.

Dreams about walking, but with pressure not registering on the soles of the feet, could be the physical stimulus for dreams about flying.

For those who are trying to escape from the realm of the feminine, either because they are trying to break away from their mothers (§ FAMILY) or because they are homosexual: The earth (§) could be a symbol of womanhood, in which case the 'flight' would be from the mother, a woman or the dreamer's own feminine characteristics.

Several of these meanings may be compressed into the one symbol, applying to different aspects of the dreamer's life. But the individual's main conflict in life, whether an inclination to remain uncommitted and idle or an obsessive ambition, should be enough to indicate the most important significance of the image.

Flying on one's own, especially far above other people, is more likely to denote ambition; flying with friends would probably indicate the desire to escape humdrum chores.

Other Creatures Flying ** Death; or the realm of angels and ghosts. *Creatures that crawl being transformed into creatures that fly:* ** The moment of death, when the body is transformed into a free-flying spirit. (A caterpillar turning into a butterfly has been used consciously in the same way as an image of the similar transformation at death.)

FOG (mist, etc.) ** A hazy obscured view; being 'fogged', befuddled; not having the 'foggiest' idea of which way to turn, etc.
Disappearing into the fog: * Death.

FOOD ** Sexual satisfaction (§ APPETITES).

Cake * A promiscuous woman: a 'tart'; lust.

Meat ** Flesh. The sensual and sexual side of living, the sins of the flesh. Death: the carcass without the living spirit. Disguised cannibalism (§).

Beef: * The strong: 'beefy'.
Bones: ** The penis, an erection.
'Chicken': * Cowardly.
'Hams': * Thighs.

Sweets * Sweetheart.

FRUIT ** Work, etc., which is 'bearing fruit'; a 'fruitful' period of development. After the flower – the blossoming of the individual – comes the fruit, that is, a later and more mature phase of the individual's life.
** Sexuality.
Elongated fruit (such as bananas): ** The phallus.
Fig, peach and other similar fruit: ** Female genitalia.
Rounded fruit (such as apples): ** The breasts.

Apple ** The fruit with which the serpent tempted Eve; love.
Stealing apples: ** Trying to procure a love that doesn't rightfully belong to the dreamer. Desire for the woman may be mixed with fear of retaliation by another man, whether her husband or father.

Watermelon * Pregnancy.

FURNITURE * The home.
Bed or mattress: ** Marriage. Or other sexual relations.
Getting out of bed: * Getting on one's feet, making one's own way (but not if the dreamer is knocked down just as he was getting up).
Carpets: * Women. It may be only their patterns (§ SHAPES) or colours (§) that are significant, however.
Chair: * 'Stool', turd.
Chest of drawers, cupboard: * A woman. *Putting an oblong or pointed object into it:* ** Intercourse.
Cupboard, closet: ** Womb, or the mind. *If it is closed:* * A closed mind or secretiveness.
Table: * A sacrificial altar. A woman.

GAMES ** The game of life. The serious conflict of life may be made into a game, possibly indicating that the dreamer is trying to make light of it. *If the dreamer won't join in the game:* ** A reluctance to become involved in the battles of life.

Ball games, athletic games, especially where the movements are rhythmical: ** The sexual act. Or the two opposing sides may represent the two sides of the conflict; in this case the ball will be the focal point, moving hither and thither as the dreamer vascillates.

Card games: May throw light on the dreamer's current conflict: for example, by emphasizing that success depends on his tactics with the cards he has, rather than relying on getting new cards.

†: The ego v. the Self. The conflict may strengthen the individual or sharpen his wits, in the dream as in life.

GARDEN ** The inner life of the individual with its flowers and fruits. Aspects of his personality that he is 'cultivating'. The various qualities of the dreamer's mind may be represented, and the dream may indicate what is being neglected. The colours (§) of the flowers (§), for example, could indicate the senses, the feelings, the intellect, or the intuitions.

The garden may be orderly or disorderly: and so may the mind.

If it is arranged in regular patterns, squares or circles: § SHAPES.

If it is overgrown with brambles or choked with weeds: * Certain features of the character are not likely to thrive in such circumstances.

If the garden is unkempt: This may reflect the dreamer's former disappointments and fear of disappointment.

** The Garden of Eden, the lost Paradise, the garden of delights: a privileged and secluded place where man and woman (Adam and Eve) hope to find harmony and love.
* Fertility and fruitfulness of body as well as of mind, therefore, the Mother (§ ARCHETYPES).

GATES May lead to the unconscious, or to the object of the dreamer's desire.
Opening a gate: * A way through to the conscious mind.
Four gates: * The four qualities of the conscious mind, of which one, for example, may be shut (§ MIND).
Garden gates: * Gates to paradise, where one may hope to encounter his heart's desire.
** The entrance to a new state of being, especially the after-death state, therefore the Gates of Heaven. People often dream of gates shortly before they die.

GESTURES There are many gestures of the body that recur in dreams as substitutes for other, more embarrassing gestures that they resemble. For example:
Repetitive back-and-forth hand or body motions: ** Coitus.
Sewing, patching, counting: ** Masturbation.
Kicking, stamping: * The movements within the womb (§); the dream could thus be about regression or fertility.

GHOSTS, Ghostly phenomena * The spiritual nature of the dream, which may refer to the individual's inner being: the Self (§ ARCHETYPES). * What is dead, extinct. *For example, a figure who leaves no footprints in the snow:* Emphasizes the fact that he is not from everyday experience.

GIANTS ** Grown-ups, usually the parents; and the dream will usually refer to the time when adults seemed gigantic to the child (§ SIZE).

GIVING *To give something the recipient dislikes in waking life:* May reveal the root of the conflict with that person, the cause of all the difficulties in the relationship: namely, the tendency to give what the dreamer wants to give rather than what the other person wants or needs. For example, a wife gave her husband strawberries, which he happened to detest in waking life though he ate them in the dream.

GOLD * Something that is precious, valuable to the dreamer; the emphasis is on value (§ TREASURE; also COLOUR).

HIDING (an object, etc.) What is it that the dreamer wishes to hide? There seems to be some inner necessity that works towards revealing a secret, making a clean breast of it, etc.; and this tendency often reveals itself first in dreams.

Dread of someone in the room watching: May relate to an incident in the past that the dreamer wouldn't have wanted witnessed.

Hiding in some dark cramped space: ** Trying to escape back into the womb (§).

HOLDING (including reaching out but finding nothing to hold onto; § NEGATIVES) * Holding the penis, masturbation.

HOLE (crater, pit) ** The womb; another small cramped space.

Crawling out of or falling through the hole: ** The entrance to the external world; being born. *Crawling into the hole:* § BIRTH. Difficulty in breathing would emphasize this meaning.

A muddy hole: ** The rectum.

Being 'in a hole': ** Being in a mess, in difficulties.

A hole anywhere in the body: ** The vagina or rectum (§ BODY).

HOME ** What is homely, normal, healthy, etc., depending very much on the individual's personal associations with home.

HOT ** The warmth of the emotions and passions, which cool with old age and death (§ FIRE).

Something hot, belonging to or associated with a particular person: ** An affection or passion for that person. *If it is scalding hot:* ** The emotion may be destructive and leave scars.

†:*Hot/Cold:* life v. death, and other opposites.

ILLNESS At best dreams may reveal the unconscious motives behind an illness, whether it is real or imaginary. These unconscious motives are sometimes diametrically opposed to the individual's conscious wishes, but in his *Book of the It* Georg Groddeck is perhaps the most convincing exponent of the idea that the unconscious 'It' has a much greater influence than the conscious will over the individual's physical health. No amount of determination will alter the course of an illness, so much as bringing to light the motives behind it; written in the deceptively simple and delightful form of letters to a young woman, in the opening letter Groddeck suggests that she may have wondered why the enormous cyst on his neck suddenly went down overnight. As soon as he realized that there was no need to display the feminine side of his personality to all and sundry with this repulsive false pregnancy on his neck, it subsided.

The unconscious motives behind an illness may vary from the wish to dominate another person or a longing for attention and loving care to a legitimate demand for rest, in which case some less significant organ may be attacked in order to preserve some more vital part, often the mind, from the effects of the individual's negligence.

There seems to be evidence that if the individual can really probe these motives, without any self-deception, he may be able to circumvent the illness itself. (Another method suggested by Groddeck for dealing with physical ills is to visualize the organ affected and address it as if it were a separate personality, tactfully but firmly inquiring why it is behaving so abominably.)

Physical illness: ** Mental worries, inner guilt, etc.

Cancer: * The Devouring Mother (§ ARCHETYPES).

Hospitals, nurses, doctors: May refer to childhood games on that theme, with their erotic overtones.

Being infected, catching germs: * Being sexually impregnated.

Ulcers: * The introvert, having failed to find any outlet for his aggression, is at war within himself.

INSECTS ** Something else that bothers the dreamer, 'bugs' him. Often, self-reproach or the pangs of conscience, which also 'pricks'. Possibly sexual thoughts, both bugs and sex being then considered dirty by the dreamer. The dream may be reminding the individual to come to terms with his conscience, which he was trying to ignore. Equally, however, the unconscious doesn't distinguish between its own guilt-ridden fantasies and real guilt, so the waking conscience may be able to dismiss its demands for self-punishment, having assessed them accurately.

* Small creatures, therefore children. *If the insects suddenly fly off:* * Children that fly, therefore dead children, in the realm of spirits (§ FLYING).

Bees * The love-mad.

Beetles If awe-inspiring: * The Self (§ ARCHETYPES).

Butterfly ** The mind, the soul, including the departed soul of someone who is dead. Also the ethereal, the beautiful. The dream could refer back to childhood and collecting butterflies or beetles. ('Psyche' is from the Greek for 'butterfly'.)

Gnats *A cloud of gnats:* * A disturbed nervous system.

Moth * The butterfly of the night: the dark, sinister aspect of the psyche.

Spider ** The feminine figure, whose affection is devouring (some female spiders devour their mates). The mother who prevents her son from getting a woman of his own, who seeks to destroy his new budding love, may be dreamed of in this form.

The web: ** The snare of home life, the domestic trap.
* Anxiety, which also ensnares and binds the individual. The strange otherness of the psychic world.
* If awe-inspiring: the Self (§ ARCHETYPES).

INVISIBLE *Figures who play a part in the dream, though the dreamer never sees them:* * Spirits. God. (§ VANISHING.)

ISLAND ** An ideal existence. ** Firm dry land in the surrounding sea of the unconscious, from which various figures may emerge. * The unborn child in the waters of the womb.

JEWELS Anything precious or of value to the individual –
often, his integrity, his individuality, his perfected inner
wholeness, which shines resplendent and is also indivisible,
incorruptible. This includes his self-confidence, his honour(?)
and his sexuality.

A 'jewel', a 'treasure' : ** A beloved person.

Jewellery : ** The women who wear jewellery and particularly
that precious part of them, their genitalia.

A jewel lying in a flower : * A union of opposites: perhaps
man and nature; or the sexual and carnal side of a man's
nature with the religious and mystical.

*Looking for jewels that turn out to be glass, especially if some
association with the dreamer's mother can be established :* ** The
idealized image of his mother has been shattered (§ FAMILY).
Or it could be some other woman who has not come up to his
expectations.

Crystal ** Hardness, purity. Illumination, especially if the
light shining in the jewel is particularly noticed. Also the
symmetry and balance of the perfected individual.

Diamond (whether seen as a jewel or as a shape (§) in the
dream) ** The whole resplendent personality: the Self. The
union of the masculine and feminine principles. Illusions are
banished. The centre of consciousness is shifted from the ego
to its original source; all energy is centred in that original,
and incorruptible, state. (Compare the Diamond Body.)
Diamonds and crystals have much the same significance as
stars (§).

Pearl ** The whole personality: mind as well as being.

Ruby May have the same significance as the rose, rose windows, mandalas (§ FLOWERS, SHAPES).

JOURNEYS * The journey through life. The individual way, or destiny. The various different types of journey, with uphill and downhill stretches, their rough and smooth patches, and so on, hardly need to be adapted at all to provide an image of the individual's progress in life, whether in his career and his ambitions, or in the various quests of his mind and his emotions. Every movement within can be reflected in a dream of moving along a road or railway tracks, across a sea or through the sky.

The dream will probably concentrate on the particular point of the dreamer's life that he has reached at the time, bringing in the periods of the past that are relevant to the current problems.

The vehicle: ** Whatever carries us through life or is keeping us going. But also the means we employ in order to reach our objective. The body, perhaps. Sometimes the types of vehicle indicate the manner in which the dreamer's life makes its way through the time allotted to it. Also relevant is whether he is alone, or with others – that is, travelling independently or collectively and gregariously; whether by his own efforts or someone else's; whether he is at the wheel and in control of which way he goes or not.

The engine: * The sexual impulse, instinct.

The destination: ** The aims, the hopes of success, the ideals of the individual, the exact nature of which will depend on how the dreamer sees his life, whether as a process of learning, a search for values, the gratification of his vanity or whatever. Often the goal can't be reached until the particular conflict to which the dreamer is currently committed has been resolved.

At the approach of death, dreams about journeys often become more meaningful, point out the way and the obstacles in the way of approaching that ultimate destination, the grave.

'Arriving', 'reaching port', etc.: ** The successful accomplishment of the aims or ambitions.

The obstacles behind: ** The past, and the difficulties, hazards and setbacks that the individual has been through; these will usually relate to his present problems and may be the direct cause of them.

The hindrances ahead : ** All the obstructions that prevent the individual from achieving his aims. His own attitude may be the cause of the biggest mental 'barriers' and 'blocks', especially at the approach of death.

'Turning corners' : ** Important events in life.

Collisions : ** Clashes, arguments, etc. Aggression or the desire for self-punishment, depending on who comes off worst.

Skilfully avoiding an accident : ** Having just enough control over one's impulses.

Trying to get a move on, but hardly moving ; for instance, putting a foot down on the accelerator and nothing happens : ** The inner conflict between ambition and laziness.

The standstill : * Deadlock; outside circumstances may be unfavourable, or perhaps some aspect of the Self is being stifled, so that the character cannot develop or mature any further; the life of the mind is stagnating.

Airplane ** A swift, and easy, journey towards the goal, without much concern for details on the way. ** Flying (§): the longing to 'lift off', get out of a rut, often to flee into the realm of the imagination. * Erection and sexual fantasies (?)

If the shape of the airplane is a cross and this is particularly noticed : § SHAPES, Cross.

An airman : ** A dream man, a man from the realm of fantasy, possibly the Animus (§ ARCHETYPES).

Bicycling ** Puberty and adolescence; also gripping the handlebars (§ HOLDING), therefore masturbation (§ RIDING).

Boats (ships, sea voyages) *** The voyage of life and of the mind, but with a broader view of the sweep of the individual's life than in dreams about buses, for example.

'Plain or smooth sailing', 'stormy crossings', 'shipwrecked' individuals : may all feature in the vivid action of the dream, but signifying what they do in colloquial speech.

Going off to sea : * Making a break with the family.

Land/the open sea : ** Security v. the hazards of independence.

Missing the boat: ** Failure to grasp the deeper implications of events.

Disembarking: ** The end of an ordeal.

Being becalmed in a sailing vessel or stuck on a sandbank: ** Stagnation, which may be the result of idleness, sloth. Such a calm may have more deadly consequences than storms or rocks.

Going down a narrow canal (or river) in a barge: ** Being born (§ BIRTH).

Ship: ** A 'vessel', a hollow receptacle, therefore a woman, or the feminine nature. * Masculinity, a man, because it is phallus-shaped and cleaves the water.

Ferry, rowboat: ** Charon's boat across the Styx, therefore death. Boats may have originated as hollowed logs for the dead which were pushed out to sea.

The Night Sea Journey ** The death of the ego. It is related to the journey across the Styx and through the underworld: overcoming the fear of death and despairing of all personal egotistic aims, which must eventually decompose like corpses.

The dreamer may be shipwrecked and devoured at some stage of the journey, but if the dream so indicates, he may emerge reborn: at one with life itself, for which corruption and putrefaction are only transformation and renewal (§ CROSSING).

Bus (a journey by bus) ** A particular short phase or stretch of the dreamer's life. Also, trying to get along just like everybody else; wanting to fit in with the rest of society, rather than pursuing some private and personal aim.

Arriving too late for the bus, missing the bus: ** The dreamer is tired, is getting behind, cannot keep up: physical exhaustion is frustrating the dreamer's desire to fit in with the outside world. Or he may be failing to adapt his life and his plans to reality, in this case the bus schedules; thus, his own arrangements must be altered if he wants to make it, to get where he wants to go.

Getting on the wrong bus, going the wrong way: ** One part of the dreamer wants to go one way, while another side of him wants to go the other way; his conflicting desires are mutually exclusive. Or circumstances may be carrying the dreamer against his will.

Overcrowded buses: ** Overcrowded professions: too many other people to compete with.

Not being able to pay the fare: ** The individual may be failing to devote his attention to the practical side of life, which may seem petty and trivial, but is necessary in order to get where he wants to go.

After a series of dreams dealing with similar frustrations, catching the bus in the right direction may be a very positive sign.

Wanting to reach home: * The desire to find one's real self. Or the hope of reaching the end of all one's difficulties: being 'home and dry'.

Car (or carriage, cart) ** Sexual 'drives': the virility and energy of the man. The impulse to get away, leave home, or move on, 'get a move on', in any other way.

In a man's dream: * A woman: 'she' goes beautifully, etc. Perhaps the dreamer's wife, mistress, sister, etc.

The body of the car: * The dreamer's body. *Something wrong with the body, or engine; if it isn't working as it should:* ** Something physically wrong with the dreamer, especially sexual troubles, but also inner problems, mental worries.

The back of the car or the back wheels: ** The dreamer's backside.

A tightly inflated tyre: * A satisfactory erection. *Running out of fuel or the fuel tank springs a leak:* * What should be the driving force has failed.

Steering or brakes not working: ** A lack of control, normally a lack of self-control, but occasionally a lack of discipline imposed from the outside.

An overloaded car or cart: ** The dreamer has taken on more than he can manage.

The contrast between two cars: May correspond to the differences between two people.

An aged, battered car: * Somebody who is aged, battered.

The many miles it had covered: ** The years behind.

Travelling in a car with one other person: ** Thoughts about marriage or an intimate relationship with another person.

Traffic violation, such as speeding, going through a red light: ** Sexual misconduct. *If this results in a collision:* ** The dreamer fears the consequences of what he is doing.

Running over pedestrians: * Fear of sadistic tendencies.

Being run over: * Fear of being raped. (The car, the motorbike or motorcycle, and the airplane are gradually replacing the horse (§ ANIMALS) as symbols of energy and sexual virility in dreams.)

Departing (departures from airports, stations, etc.) ***
Death: 'departing this world'. Freud saw all journeys as reminders of death; and certainly if there is any mention of the word 'departing' or 'departure', the journey is likely to have this significance.

Missing the train, not reaching this final destination: ** Reassurance from the unconscious that there is still time left; there is no need to panic or hurry.

After losing some beloved person, people often have recurring dreams of being on a train: ** The impulse to join their beloved in death. When this impulse has been confronted consciously and some attempt has been made to come to terms with it, the dreams will stop.

The time of departure: ** The hour of death.

Journeys to the West: * Death: 'going West' or 'gone West'.

Driving ** The dreamer's drives and cravings in particular, as well as the general significance of journeys.

If the dreamer drives: ** Independence and mastery over his destiny. *If he drives carelessly:* ** Losing control over his sexual instincts.

If he is driven by someone else: ** Dependence on someone else. If he is too passive and has little or no say in the direction his life is taking, he may well be driven in the wrong direction and end up in some unpleasant situation.

If someone else takes the wheel: ** A change from the active to the passive role.

Overtaking: ** The dreamer 'taking over', taking control and altogether playing a more prominent part in life. 'Getting ahead'.

Being overtaken: Other people or other forces controlling or taking possession of the dreamer. The way people behave in traffic often reveals an inner symbolic attitude towards the outside world, trying to 'get ahead', as in dreams.

Roads ** The individual way or destiny, which leads to the realization of one's aims and objectives.

A stretch of road: ** A period of time; the part already covered being the past, while the future is the road that lies ahead.

A choice of roads: ** Alternative courses of action.

†*High road/low road:* * The idealistic way v. the selfish way.

Where the roads fork, divide: * Parting from someone or from old ways. Or a cleavage; legs also form a V, therefore perhaps a woman.

A crossroads: * A union of opposites, the meeting of two conflicting ways.

A turn in the road: * New events lie ahead.

A track, off to one side of the road: ** Being 'side-tracked' from one's objective. Or 'going off the beaten track' to try something unusual or original.

A cul-de-sac or dead end: ** A road that leads nowhere.

Going up steep hills: ** States of tension arising from work(?) or sexual exertions(?). *If the effort is too much for the dreamer and he is not likely to reach the top:* He is asking too much of himself or of the world.

Going 'downhill': ** The dreamer is letting himself go and may be in danger of losing control. The rest of the dream should indicate whether it is in relation to sex, gambling or whatever.

The dreamer's unconscious view of his destiny may differ drastically from his conscious view, and this could be a cause of conflict and needless waste of energy.

Motorbike, motorcycle (§ RIDING): A phallic symbol of masculine vitality, youth and instinct.

Trains ** All that is vigorous and go-ahead in the dreamer. His vitality and passions, his sexual mechanism. ** The individual's progress. * 'Trains of thought'.

Missing the train: ** Fear of missing an opportunity, something critical; failing to make the progress he'd hoped for. There may no longer be enough energy to catch hold of life and make a success of it, or the dreamer may be too anxious about getting ahead too fast and so spoil his chances, especially if he's been held back in the past.

Trying to get off the train: ** The dreamer is afraid of reaching his destination, afraid of an anticlimax; or perhaps the pace is too much for him.

†: Both missing a train, which may be arranged by the dreamer's unconscious, and trying to get off the train may signify a regressive tendency, a shrinking from life rather than facing it, tackling it and moving with it: progress v. regress.

Mixed feelings about taking that particular journey: * Confusion and inner turmoil about leaving home, or taking on new responsibilities, and so on.

Catching the train: An effort that has met with success. Ideally, after missing trains, the dreamer may start catching the trains later in the series of dreams, and later still may drive them.

A single track: ** The individual is being too 'one-tracked' (§ SHAPES, Lines).

'Getting derailed' and 'getting back on the right track', etc.: May all feature in the vivid pictorial language of dreams as dramatic events.

Safety valves hissing steam: * Emission.

The dreamer having to get off the train too soon: * Premature ejaculation.

The station: A woman; and the dreamer may draw up at the platform or hurtle through.

Arriving at a station: * Death (§ JOURNEYS, Departing).

Walk ** Progressing slowly but by one's own energy, not depending on any external aid.

Going for a walk: * Aimless wandering through life.

KEY ** The 'key' to some problem; the solution of a difficulty. The 'key' to happiness, and possibly someone who is that key. * 'The keys of the kingdom.' ** A phallus, and therefore a man, because of the way it operates. 'A key in a dream to him which would marry, signifieth a good and handsome wife' (Artemidorus).

KILLING (§ AGGRESSION, CRIME, DEATH, SACRIFICE).
Killing animals: § ANIMALS.
Killing a parent: § FAMILY.
The figure whom the dreamer is killing may be a personification of some part of himself that he is trying to stifle, choke, strangle, etc. In this case it will be important to come to terms consciously with this aspect of himself that he dislikes so much. As with animals, if he did destroy it, he would certainly destroy other vital forces along with it; if he can face this part of himself, however unpleasant at first glance, by coming to understand the forces at work within him, he may be able to transform them.

KISS * Conquest and assimilation (§ SEX).

LADDER ** The social 'ladder'. Jacob's ladder to heaven. Going up and down, therefore intercourse.

LANGUAGES (foreign) ** Something the dreamer does not understand about himself. Anything that is foreign, mis-understood. Occasionally the symbolic language of the dream itself, which is like a riddle in a foreign tongue. *Especially German or any language that might be associated with 'the enemy':* ** Apprehension.

A LETTER
Unopened: * Virginity.
Opening a letter: * Defloration.
Not reading a letter: * Ignorance, ignoring.

LIGHT ** Conscious intellect, or insight.
A beam of bright light directed at someone or something in particular: ** The conscious attention of the dreamer should be directed that way. *If directed at the dreamer:* ** He should become more aware of himself: know his own motives; stop attributing to others qualities that aren't theirs at all but are extensions of his own delusions and limitations.
Insufficient light: ** A 'dim, murky' and inadequate under-standing of whatever the dreamer is trying to see.
A dazzling light: ** Too much conscious knowledge may blind the knower to all that lies in the shadows, especially of the unconscious.

A bright white light (if it resembles moonlight): * The spirit, the intuition (§ MOON).

LOSE
Losing something or getting lost: ** Being mentally distracted. Going astray. *Finding the object again, or finding the way:* * The difficult period is over.
Losing an object that resembles the phallus: * Fear of castration (§).

LUGGAGE (baggage) Marriage (§ PACKING).

MACHINERY ** Mechanical behaviour: the habit-ridden automaton. The body, its mechanics, the way it works.
Many bits of machinery such as oiled pistons, etc.: ** Sexual activities.
A steam engine: * The stomach.
Elaborate mechanism: ** The most complex part of the body, the brain; therefore complicated problems in that realm.
Taking the mechanism to bits: ** Exposing the individual's inner workings, motives and conflicts, trying to get at whatever is faulty.
The mechanic: * The doctor.
The inventor: * God.

MASK ** The individual's façade, or persona.
Being unable to remove the mask: ** The individual risks becoming identified with his façade: if he refuses to show his real face, his true personality may be stifled and wither away for lack of contact with the outside world and lack of response from other people (§ CLOTHES, Being overdressed).

MATCHSTICK * The penis.
Striking the match and the flame bursting forth: ** Intercourse.

MILL * The mills of God, 'which grind slowly but grind exceedingly small'.

MIND *From the Unconscious to the Conscious.* The mind has been divided into conscious and unconscious simply for the convenience of commentators. This doesn't mean that there are two separate parts of the mind operating in different ways; it is just a way of distinguishing between those mental operations of which we are aware and may even consciously will, and those we ignore but that continue to operate and may even influence our lives drastically. In the unconscious are all kinds of motivations we don't acknowledge, as well as vital forces (§ ARCHETYPES). This is the background as well as the source of all our thoughts and actions. We may derive great energy and peace from being in accord with it and experience considerable frustration if we try to go against it.

Dreams are messages from the unconscious to the conscious. *The Four Functions of the Mind.*

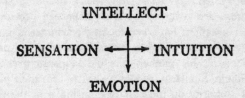

Most people have one dominant function, two that are auxiliary, and one that is inferior. The inferior function is usually the one opposite the dominant faculty (as shown in the diagram): the intellectual may often neglect his emotional life, for example. But it is only by developing the inferior function later in life that the individual can restore the balance of his personality. Buried as it is in the inner being, it also remains fresh and spontaneous, which makes it invaluable for recovering one's original wonder at life.

Dreams may indicate the need to pay attention to this fourth neglected function, so that the individual can fulfil the whole of his potential (§ COLOURS; NUMBERS, Three and Four). If he does so, symbols of wholeness may appear in later dreams.

'Repression', 'Inhibitions'. Hardly any idea in psychology has been so misrepresented as 'repression', which consists of disregarding certain inner factors. Like facts in the outside world, inner factors don't disappear merely because you ignore them; on the contrary, as soon as the individual turns

his back on them his inner nature, and particularly its more unpleasant aspects, is left completely free to condition his responses and so govern many of his actions. It is only by becoming 'uninhibited' – that is to say, recognizing the forces at work within him – that the individual himself gains control of the situation and becomes for the first time able to make conscious delusion-free decisions about his life.

Dreams will reveal the dreamer's unconscious wishes, aggressions, emotions and so on that could reveal the motives behind many of his actions. For example, recognizing 'piglike' qualities, far from meaning that one is becoming more piglike, is the first stage in reckoning with and overcoming them (§ ANIMALS, Pig).

Fixed Patterns of Behaviour. Many of our responses to situations are governed by what happened previously in a similar situation; but when the new encounter is only superficially the same – as when a man meets another woman who in fact isn't his mother – the old response may be quite unsuitable. Similarly, people are apt to base their judgement of all authority on the past relationship with the father (or lack of father).

Dreams often recall relevant incidents from the past that may be affecting the individual's present decisions, or even warping his life.

MIRRORS ** Narcissism, which is basically egotistic and petty, and may be autoerotic or homosexual. This can nevertheless be cultivated by conscious effort into a knowledge of Self as a part of creation and an image of that creation, and people who are narcissistic in this way are sometimes the most creative.

Reflections: The mind also 'reflects' on its own nature. The unconscious is occasionally represented as the mirror opposite the conscious mind in which everything is distorted in looking-glass language.

The reflection of ourselves: * How we are seen by others and therefore our façade, or persona. The object and its reflection are in fact always one and the same thing. So the unconscious may use this image to point out the fundamental unity between two things that the dreamer has been deluded into thinking of as separate or different. Plato recommended the mirror to young people for observing the progress of virtue, or viciousness, visible in their own faces (§ WATER, Reflections).

MONEY *** Anything of equivalent value, often time or energy, sometimes love.

A certain sum of money: ** So many days.

Being short of money: ** Being short of time or not having enough energy, or both. An unreasonable anxiety about money in old age, in people who are perfectly well off, is often really a disguised concern about their failing energy and the lack of time left to them. The irrational nature of their thrift and frugality points to its source in the unconscious (§ BODY, Hair).

Being unwilling to split up a large note in order to get small change: ** Being unwilling to divide one's energies for the sake of a whole lot of trivialities. This attitude often results in achieving nothing at all. The note becomes the individual's great potential, which is never spent, never made actual.

The charge is excessive: ** The amount of effort involved is too great. Or the individual will have to 'pay' for what he does. *To 'pay':* ** To suffer later.

Passing off counterfeit money: ** Cheating, and therefore not giving true value in any sphere of life, especially in relationships involving love. The individual who has cheated someone often becomes obsessed with the idea of being cheated himself; the dream could be trying to point out that it is he who was the cheat originally and that is the actual cause of his obsession.

Squandering money: * Wasting potential love in promiscuity, masturbation, etc.

The father or husband who refuses money: ** He is withholding his love.

Something that is cheap: * Shoddy, 'cheap' behaviour.

MOON ** The realm of the feminine, the maternal, including the unconscious soul. The opposite of the sun (§) and the reflection of it (§ MIRRORS), this light-in-the-dark often refers to direct intuitive knowledge shining in the depths of the unconscious. If this purely intuitive understanding is honoured, it may become the source of all spiritual wisdom; if not, then madness – 'lunacy' – may overpower the individual.

The New Moon and the Full Moon: * Magic and madness.

The phases of the moon: * The menstrual cycle. Change, and flux of the cyclic tides of life.

The moon growing full: * Pregnancy.

In a man's dream: * His Anima (§ ARCHETYPES).

In a woman's dream, because the moon is a symbol of all that is opposite to the conscious daylight world, all that is mysterious, strange and other-worldly: * Her Animus.

** Death and resurrection; the image of renewal through a process of transformation, because the moon wanes and is extinguished, only to be reborn with the New Moon. That this is known to result from the play of light on the unchanging moon doesn't alter the image that points to a changeless immortality underlying the superficial changes and transformations.

Trying to reach the moon, 'reaching for the moon': Desire, yearning for the unattainable. The date of Easter is determined by the cycles of the moon and is thus related to this symbolic significance.

Moonlit landscapes: * A refuge where lovers can dream before facing harsh realities.

* Feminine frailty or fickleness. Weakness and submission. Rhythm, change and fruitfulness (§ SHAPES, Crescent).

MOUNTAINS (Hills) ** Obstacles and difficulties that could be regarded as a challenge. The dreamer may be exaggerating his difficulties – 'making a mountain out of a molehill'.

The mountain-top or hill-top: ** The 'peak' of the individual's ambitions, the 'height' of his powers or of his success. His experience and knowledge. The goal.

Climbing mountains: * The first half of life, when the difficulties must be overcome in order to reach the peak.

Struggling to scale insurmountable heights and not getting anywhere: ** The dreamer is wasting his energy on unattainable goals; it could be better spent in other directions, as may be indicated by the dream. Otherwise this conceit, which makes him so demanding of himself, may have disastrous consequences (§ CLIMBING).
Descending: * The second half of life.

* Parts of the body.
Mountain ledge: ** The bosom.
Being in the valley between high mountains: ** Protection, security, comfort, which can easily turn to isolation and imprisonment.

MUSEUMS ** A store of memories.

MUSIC * The music of life, with its harmonies and discords. Also, 'facing the music', and 'playing on the emotions'.
The Organ: ** The male organ. *The Organist:* * A personification of the male organ, and of the sex life of the individual.
Orchestra: ** The dreamer's mind, and especially his emotions, with which music is closely associated.
Discordant notes: * An underlying conflict; the rest of the dream may point to its source.

MYTH A great deal of light can be thrown on dreams by comparing them with myths. And if a particular dream has anything in common with some myth – especially if that myth springs to mind spontaneously shortly after waking or while thinking about the dream – the individual may discover a hidden fund of meaning in his dream by drawing analogies with the myth.

Being NAKED ** The individual's desire to remove his façade, or persona (§ CLOTHES); to drop all pretences and be himself for a change. But this will also make him defenceless. This desire on the part of the dreamer to be less secretive, less on the defensive, more open and frank may be with regard to one particular person, someone with whom he wishes to get beyond mere social formalities; or it may be directed at someone who has misunderstood his outward behaviour.

Being 'stripped down' to the 'bare' facts, the 'naked' truth, etc.: ** Exposing his natural instincts and sexuality, which are also part of his true self; letting his repressed longings be known. Also revealing his inadequacy or shortcomings; a feeling of inferiority or guilt.

Especially if the dream is accompanied by a feeling of shame: § EMOTIONS.

If everybody disapproves: ** The dreamer fears that if he lets others see him as he really is, dares to be himself, they will disapprove. *If nobody minds or takes any notice:* ** An attempt on the part of the unconscious to rectify the individual's exaggerated self-consciousness. Or the dreamer himself doesn't care, perhaps determinedly, about his outward appearance or the effect he has on others.

Everyone or no one disapproves: May have been inserted into the dream to represent the dreamer's own attitude towards his own behaviour. *Particular people:* Are more likely to represent what others really think or might think.

†: The fear of being embarrassed by others may just express the other side of the dreamer's inner conflict: the longing to expose himself v. the fear of doing so.

* A desire to attract attention to his own body, to be an exhibitionist. The individual may have become unduly shy and reserved as a result of some childhood act of exhibitionism for which he was reprimanded. The dream could be trying to bring this to light so that it can be consciously dismissed as irrelevant.

* The wish to be a child again, when running around naked didn't matter.

NEGATIVES ** The dreamer's wish that things were not as they are. Negatives as such are not valid in dreams. Trying to deny the existence of a thought is often an attempt to keep the anxiety it arouses under control; hence whatever the dream claims is 'not' there has in fact entered the dreamer's mind, but he wishes it hadn't.

Someone whose absence is noticed, who isn't there: ** Somebody who is there, playing a part in the dream, but whose presence is painful to the dreamer.

NIGHTMARE A nightmare expresses an intense mental conflict that probably centres on some form of repressed sexual desire. The less this desire is acknowledged, the greater the fear that accompanies it – and it is this fear that turns an erotic dream into a nightmare. The nightmare is the epitome of *Angst*, and from it the cause and nature of the individual's dread may be discovered.

The fear, which is the main feature of the nightmare: ** Inner guilt, often arising from an illicit, and therefore inhibited, desire.

Pressure on the chest or breast that makes it difficult to breathe, or an inability to move: ** The self-surrender in the act of intercourse, with the dreamer in the passive role.

Sadism and aggressions: * Love combined with guilt and fear.

The unknown being: * The individual towards whom the love/hate is directed.

Where this desire is incestuous, the intense feeling of inner guilt has occasionally led to its obvious punishment, which is impotence. It was in this particular field that incubation dreams were so successful, warding off and relieving the sense of guilt by religious rites; transferring the guilt to the lewd demon and exorcising it. The process hasn't changed, only the words: the libido is now the lewd demon, for which the individual should not feel too responsible. There is no need to find the solution to the insoluble conflict. All that matters is to know, whether in real or symbolic form, the process that is at work. Like fear of the dark, the morbid dread can be dispelled by turning on the light or opening one's eyes and looking at the figures and emotions involved as they really are. The fear is also a safeguard that could be rendered superfluous once the conscious will is properly directed.

The nightmares of early childhood, which may recur later in life, could refer to the experience of being born, especially if certain details of the nightmare can be related to the details of actual birth (§).

NUMBERS The numbers in dreams are often surprisingly accurate and may provide a reliable clue as to what the dream is really about, once the individual has understood the curious way in which the unconscious mind seems to enjoy juggling with numbers.

The unconscious calendar: Numbers in dreams often refer to significant dates, but the unconscious remembers dates that have long eluded the conscious mind, whether birthdays and the age of the dreamer or other anniversaries that are significant to him for some reason.

A certain number of things: ** Something quite different, the only common feature being the number: for example, five sentences could signify five visits. Sums of money, dates, numbers of miles, etc., are all interchangeable – for example, twenty-five minutes could refer to £25.

A number of identical objects: * The same act repeated: the same event that has occurred often. Or could be emphasizing the significance of the object in the dream: this is one way the unconscious mind repeats a word, as if to say, I've told you again and again.

A certain number of people: ** The number of people in the dreamer's family or some other group that is equally significant to him. The relationship between the figures in the dream may then be taken as referring to the relationship between members of the family or other group as seen by the dreamer's unconscious.

Even numbers: ** The feminine.

Odd numbers: ** The masculine. Or the peculiar, 'odd' and sometimes morally wrong.

Numbers one to nine: * Stages on the way to the complete zero or circle (§ SHAPES). The unconscious does play with numbers, however, and it may be necessary to divide them up into parts that then add or occasionally multiply together in order to discover the significant factors. These may be discovered by spontaneous associations or by comparing numbers that are significant to the dreamer with the numbers in the dream, etc. (For One, Two, Three and Four, Five, Six: § SHAPES, Lines, Triangle, Square, Star.) People have always felt especially deeply about the symbolic significance of numbers and often attribute personal meanings to particular numbers, which may play a part in dreams.

One ** The phallic shape, and therefore the masculine, perhaps a man. Or isolation. Or 'Number One', Me. Or oneness, unity.

Two ** Duality; the two sides or two halves of anything. Often the masculine and the feminine: a 'pair', a 'couple', therefore a harmonious heterosexual relationship. Two objects, two houses, especially where one is contrasted with the other in some way: Either/or. A choice and often a conflict between the two – two people(?). Often an inner split: two different outlooks on the world, two different attitudes towards something. The conscious and unconscious attitudes may be contrasted, or the light and the dark, the altruistic and the selfish, etc.

One in front of the other: * Progress, growth, transformation.

Two parallel roads or railway tracks: ** Being heterosexual or homosexual: being married or being a bachelor, etc. * Sharing or halving. * 'Number Two': excrement (§ BODY).

Two and a Half ** Father, mother and child.

Three ** The male genitals. Father, mother and child. The

Trinity. *For example, three parcels of waste paper:* * The dreamer considered the doctrine of the Trinity to be rubbish.

Three and Four ** The four faculties of the mind (§), of which one has been neglected, and is therefore the individual's most vulnerable point. Especially three animals, and then a fourth, which is somehow distinguished from the others.

Four ** Wholeness: all four faculties of the mind are satisfactorily integrated into the whole personality.
Four people: ** The individual still depends on other people, possibly his family (§), in order to complement and complete his experience of life.
A more abstract representation of four, such as fourfold lightning, a square, etc.: ** The individual is discovering the whole range of sensual, intellectual, emotional and intuitive experience within himself. Or the three aspects of the Godhead – being, consciousness and love – plus matter and the realm of the feminine. ** Order. Such ordered divisions as the four seasons, the four points of the compass and so on. Or the four elements, which correspond to the four temperaments.

Four and Five * Ideal spiritual goals v. natural corporeal aims.

Five ** Nature: the flesh, the body, which has five appendages with its head, arms and legs, as the hand has five fingers. Life.

Six ** Sex, not only because it is phonetically similar, but also because it is the multiplication of 3×2, the male and the female, and so has become a sign of generation and evolution. *If the six is upside down:* ** Sexual and emotional upheaval.

Seven * The seventh day, a day devoted to God. The number of archangels of Jewish tradition and of the planetary gods of the ancients. It is generally a sacred number by tradition.

Eight Apparently has no symbolic significance, except possibly as 2×4 (§ FOUR, above).

Nine ** The nine months of pregnancy. ** The peak of achievement, being the highest digit.

Ten ** Male and female; intercourse; marriage. * The Commandments (another particular number may specify which one).

Zero Except for its pictorial significance as a female symbol or as a circle, the unconscious disregards zeros and decimal points. (For example, 3.25 P.M. = 32·5 (32½) years old: § TIME.)

100: * Two female elements to one male: two women and one man.

Twelve ** Time: the twelve hours of the day, the twelve months of the year, the twelve signs of the zodiac. A climax or culminating point.

Twenty-four The hours of the day.

Seventy * Seventy years, and therefore an average lifetime.

¼ * 'Quarters': home.

½ * Halfway.

OBJECTS (Things) Conflicts, relationships and especially sexual fantasies become less accurately embarrassing, or less painful, if they are seen in terms of objects. People or ideas may also be reified. Just as the bee and its honeycomb are both a part of nature, so dreams don't seem to differentiate between natural and the man-made objects.

All long, oblong or pointed objects; anything that expands, collapses, penetrates, squirts or ejects; or any object that resembles the phallus in some other way, such as beams, poles, pens, hose, rope, etc.; anything that is manipulated or played on (for example, instruments): ******* The phallus. Sometimes drawing a curious object that features in a dream, for example an odd table lamp, will reveal its obvious resemblance to the male genitals. A sharp pointed instrument could also signify the 'needle' of intellect, but if it also emits something, as a syringe does, then it will almost certainly refer to the penis. *A broken pencil, etc.:* ****** Castration (§). *A slanting beam, especially if it is in the way of the dreamer as he tries to get near to a woman:* ****** Homosexuality, or some other 'slant' on sex.

All hollow or circular objects; containers and vessels of any kind; for example, bags, cups, caves, loops, hoops, etc.: ******* Female genitalia, therefore the woman, or the feminine nature. Or the womb and therefore specifically the mother, or mother archetype (§). This significance is often emphasized by other associations, such as the woman with the kitchen, so that ovens and cooking vessels are a particularly common image of womanhood. So is a woman's handbag. *A cup, goblet or chalice:* ****** The vagina, woman. ****** The whole personality. *If it is cracked:* ***** Weak points in the character. *Two cups:* ***** The contrast between the Mother and the Terrible Mother (§ARCHETYPES). 'Emptiness is a great feminine secret' (Jung).

Objects made of material – matter, 'mater' – such as wood, cloth, paper: ** The mother, or motherhood.
A rug: * A woman.
Hardware: * Imperishable memories.
Objects that are alive: * Images of impressions or memories of the past that are still alive within the dreamer, still playing a part in his life. *Objects coming to life:* ** New life, new potentialities developing within the dreamer (§ STATUES).
Geometrically shaped objects: § SHAPES.

OBSTACLES *Such as walls, fences, locked doors, brakes, or possibly something like rain preventing the individual from going out, etc.:* *** Inhibitions, conscience or some other form of restraint or intervening difficulty. But also, reluctance on the part of the dreamer, since he has introduced the obstacles into the dream. Unconsciously, the dreamer may be aware of the hazards and risk involved in achieving his conscious aims, realizing ambitions that may then threaten personal relationships, etc. The obstacles in the dream may refer to actual difficulties that he only pretends to abhor, but unconsciously instigates. However, this failure to reconcile conscious aims with the unconscious outlook can lead to deadlock and sterility.

OCCUPATIONS In dreams, as in childhood, all occupations are very much lumped together as an entity: one may stand for another, and all just represent man in his official capacity, his corporate identity. Like clothes (§) they may refer to his persona, or façade (§ PEOPLE).

OGRE * The father (§ ARCHETYPES).

OPPOSITE § POSITION.

OPPOSITES (Antitheses, contrasts) It is important to

search out the opposites and contrasts in dreams, for these will often throw light on the individual's inner tensions and conflicts. Most dream images could be paired off by opposites, and when the opposing images occur in a particular dream, their significance should become clear if they are juxtaposed and related to the individual's waking life.

A few examples may help to illustrate the way in which the unconscious uses contrasting images to state both sides of the problem pictorially: *hot/cold, summer/winter, south/north:* ** Love, warmth v. indifference, dislike. *Sun/moon, king/queen, emperor/empress:* ** masculine v. feminine. *Old/new (whether something old in contrast with something new, or an old house or apartment compared with a new one, etc.):* * old attitudes v. new attitudes. *Volatile/solid, air/earth, eagle/toad:* ** spirit v. flesh and material considerations. *Fire/water:* ** active v. passive. *Exterior/interior, outer/inner:* *** extrovert and façade v. introvert and inner man. *Walking/driving:* * making slow progress (but by one's own steam) v. moving fast (but depending on supports, aids). *Dark/light, black/white, above/below, sweet/bitter:* ** the pure, the idealistic v. the immoral, compulsive.

Animals are often contrasted. For example, bear/wolf: ** mother v. harlot. (In a particular instance this pointed to the individual's childish longing to stay with and be pampered by her mother, battling with her inner need to take on a new, intensely personal love relationship involving responsibilities.) § CONFLICT.

OVEN ** Womb: A woman has two children and one 'in the oven'.

PACKING (a suitcase, etc.) ** 'Packing' things into one's life, making the most of one's time.
'Putting something away' in a case, etc.: * Putting something out of mind: deliberately ignoring it, forgetting about it or hiding it from others.

PALMS * Traditional symbols of valour, triumph, victory; also carried in the triumphal procession of Palm Sunday.

PAPER ** Some more significant piece of paper.
A sheet of blank paper: ** An important letter that the dreamer has sent or received.

Being **PARALYSED** (rooted to the spot, unable to move, frozen, immobile) *** Conflicting impulses or emotions. The dreamer is longing to do something but is immobilized by fear of the consequences. Or, conversely, he longs to flee from whatever is pursuing him, but because he unconsciously desires it he can't move because he doesn't want to.

This conflicting emotion of desire and wanting to face something, but at the same time longing to flee from it, often arises where there is a strong sexual attraction mingled with disgust. The physical inability to move signifies a mental block or inhibition – some aspect of the character is unwilling to move. If on the other hand the individual is torn between ambition and laziness, the dream may refer to that.
What the dreamer can't do in the dream: ** What he is unwilling to do, refuses to do in life. And is also a valid image of the horrors of stagnation.

If the dream comes at a time when the individual is challenging the authority of his parents or whatever else he has accepted without questioning for himself: ** The dream may refer to the fear and dread involved in continuing to go his own way: his rigidly established concepts from the past impede his free movement. He has been moulded.

Especially if just a limb is paralysed: ** Impotence, therefore emotional stagnation. A rigid outlook or a lack of confidence could also be the cause of the individual's inability to 'make a move' (§ STIFF). The same emotional conflict, in a more acute form, could be the cause of psychosomatic paralysis.

PASSPORT ** A means of identification, a way of establishing who 'I' am: and therefore may refer to the ego (§ ARCHE-TYPES).

PEN ** Penis. * Writing.

PEOPLE The people who figure in dreams – if they're not simply playing themselves – may be playing one of three main roles: they may represent somebody who is more significant to the dreamer; they may be there for one aspect of their character only, and so represent the dreamer's ideas (for example, the unconscious may illustrate its ideas about marriage, through the 'typical married couple'); they may represent the dreamer's own inner life, as if projected on to a screen.

If the dreamer is emotionally involved with the people who figure in his dreams, or has any form of vital relationship with them in life, whether loving or antagonistic, then there's no need to look for any abstruse explanation of why he's dreaming about that person. But when the individual can't understand what some mere acquaintance is doing in his dreams at all, then that person will invariably stand for somebody else or something else. Even the dream figure's sex may be switched in order to conceal the true identity. Since the disguise is adopted, it is more than likely that the true identity of the dream figure, and whatever the dream has to say about him or her, will be of a disconcerting nature to the dreamer.

Fortunately, there is usually some clue to help unmask the figure in the dream: he will invariably have something in common with the person who is actually implicated. Some striking physical feature, such as fair hair or blue eyes, may lead the individual by way of association to whoever was really in the leading role underneath the makeup. Or it could be his expression that gives him away: if the dream figure is severe-looking, it may remind the individual of somebody who looks severe. He may use a word or a phrase that was actually used only the other day by the true subject of the dream. Sometimes it is a bit of the dream figure's clothing or his background or the setting of the dream that reveals his true identity. It could also be the nationality of the dream figure: for example, Franklin Roosevelt once represented an altogether different American, with whom the dreamer was involved at the time.

Somebody else's mother, father, brother, etc.: ** The dreamer's own parent or relation.

In a series of dreams, many different people with walk-on parts: May all represent the same one person who is significant to the dreamer. The same is true of one dream figure, especially if there are certain irreconcilable aspects to his presence in the dream, such as if one minute he is dead and the next alive: he may be two or more people lumped together into the one figure, mother and wife, for instance.

Three people (the dreamer, plus one man and one woman): Is as common a theme in dream as in movies. It concerns originally the love for one parent and rivalry with the other, but eventually becomes the basic pattern of other relationships and rivalries.

A figure from the past: * That period in the dreamer's past. Some other figure from the dreamer's past, who matters more to him.

As is true of all dream images, the particular figure chosen as a substitute for the real protagonist of the dream is not selected arbitrarily. Often, indeed, the choice throws considerable light on the dreamer's attitude to the person who is really figuring in the dream. The images themselves are often more revealing than the underlying 'meaning' of the dream, but not until their true bearing on the individual's life has been discovered. To dream of somebody as an emperor, for example, is revealing only after the individual knows whom it is that he thinks so highly of.

Dreams give a totally subjective view of the individual's loves and hates. 'If you want to know who's dreaming about you, consult your own dreams' (Hall). But we are most likely to dream about people when there is a conflict between affection and antagonism. People about whom we are indifferent or for whom we have unmixed affection don't figure much in dreams, except as codes.

Someone may take part in a dream solely as the representative of one facet of that particular person's character or one aspect of his life.

Often in dreams there may be a noted contrast between two of the participants, to illustrate the two sides of the dreamer's thoughts on a particular subject, for example: *One of the figures in the dream may be practical while the other is dreamy; one tidy, the other sloppy; one overbearing, the other insignificant; one upright and moral, the other debauched and vicious; one enlightened and reasonable, another rigid and dogmatic:* *** The dreamer's contrasting thoughts about being efficient and practical, in contrast with being dreamy and poetic, etc.

Similarly, other people's circumstances may be contrasted: bachelors, homosexuals, and divorced people as opposed to married people; successful people in contrast with failures; somebody who has just had an abortion appearing in the same dream as somebody with lots of children: *** The dreamer is toying with these ideas, homosexuality, marriage, abortion, etc.

Composite figures made up of several people known to the dreamer, or one person transforming into another or merging indistinctly with another: Very often emphasizes the fact that the people are there only as figments of an idea; if all the different people have one thing in common – for example, if they are all divorced – then the dream will be trying to attract the dreamer's attention to the idea of divorce. Or the fact that these various people have something in common may be trying to throw light on what the dreamer thinks of one of them in particular (all the others will be like pictorial adjectives).

In the first part of life other people are experienced at simple face value and become part of a personal concrete imagery, with the inevitable danger that young people often confuse their fantasies about other people with reality, and are deluded – for example, when the beloved is only an idea inside the youth's head, bearing little or no relation to the actual person. This situation only gets worse in later life unless the inner realm is recognized for what it is, so that the individual can allow for its powerful influence on his outlook. At the same time this enables him to realize that what he sees of others is only the outward expression of their inner being. This changing attitude, or the need for change, is often reflected in dreams and especially in the type of figures who play a part in them.

'Dreams are absolutely egoistic' (Freud). And if the figures in them don't relate to people with whom the dreamer is intensely involved or to ideas that are of direct concern to himself, they will probably be projections and personifications of his own inner life. (Public figures can never be significant enough in themselves to feature in the individual's dreams, unless they can be adapted to fit his particular concerns.)

Various figures are the most vivid and accurate images of the forces at work within each individual, the most important of which are the archetypes (§). But the dreamer will also attribute to other figures tendencies that are really his own in order to avoid embarrassment or, occasionally, in order to assess the situation more objectively. But it is usually the unacceptable part of his own personality that the dreamer rejects in this way, like a child spitting out what it doesn't like. Thus someone else or some purely fictitious figure may be attributed with the dreamer's own hypocritical tendencies, etc., while the dreamer himself feels duly disgusted.

Just as parts of the character can be personified, so can parts of the dreamer's body. For example, *A man:* * His penis. *If he is impoverished, sick, or wounded:* * Impotence. A particular illness may figure in dreams as a person, with particular demands made on the individual, etc.

It may be fruitful for a woman to adapt freely some of the figures who appear in this section. By recognizing the principles at work, even though the particular images were taken from a man's dream and the interpretation here accords with his particular circumstances, it may still have some bearing or throw some light on other figures who appear in her dreams. Thus if an actress appears in a woman's dream, it would be well worth consulting ACTOR to see if the material presented there is relevant to her dream, as well as referring to FILM STAR.

Often it is only by making full use of approximate images that the real meaning of the dream comes to light.

Actor ** An artificial personality, and therefore the dreamer himself behaving in an artificial manner; often his persona.

Ancestors (including grandparents) ** Concern about roots and background. Often the imperatives of childhood, conscience. Ancestors are traditionally the guardians of good manners and behaviour as well as of deeper moral and religious values. * Parents, in a distorted form because the dream is dealing with loves and antagonism that might prove disconcerting to the dreamer.

Authorities (such as judges, teachers, etc.) ** The individual's concept of authority, which will have been based largely on his relationship with his father. If the father was unreliable, egocentrically demanding or believed in discipline regardless of whether it had any point or bore any fruit, then authority inevitably becomes identified with treachery, exploitation, etc., and is rejected out of hand, even where it may be appropriate. The old attitude is projected on to each new situation. Recurring dreams about authorities may be calling the dreamer's attention to this or to some equivalent problem. (§ ARCHETYPES, Father/Ogre.) ** The conscience within, therefore often the authority of God. The conscious mind, which has the ultimate responsibility for decisions.

Baby ** The birth of new potentialities within the individual. * His bondage to childishness.
'Passing the baby': * Getting rid of responsibilities, passing them on to someone else.

Boy (whether a boy known to the dreamer or not) ** The dreamer himself, when he was a boy, boyhood; that period of his life or a part of his personality, a part of his potential that has been left behind on the way. The dream could be urging the individual to bear his younger self in mind, and form some kind of relationship with the boy he used to be, in order to avoid certain pitfalls that would come from ignoring or rejecting his own past. * The Self (§ ARCHETYPES). But still young and growing, immature, but with the potential of further development (§ PEOPLE, Child).

Butcher * Aggression (§). * Sacrifice (§).

Chemist * Poison (§).

Child (who could be one of the dreamer's own children) ** The child within the dreamer, and all the promise associated with that childhood. The childlike nature.

Once the individual has emerged from childhood and no longer identifies himself with the child, he may relate to the child in himself with considerable profit, especially in the bringing up of children, for example. There is a vast difference between the parents who are still childish, the Victorian type who have utterly rejected their childhood, and those who are wholly adult but have a rapport and dialogue with their own childhood self and thus are able to understand their children without becoming a grotesque imitation of a child in a child's eyes.

* The beginnings of new life within, which, as the acorn contains the potential oak, already contains the potential of wholeness, the Self (§ ARCHETYPES).

* The unity of opposites: the way in which the mother and the father, without losing any of their own individuality, become one in the child, may be an image of the way it is possible to grow beyond conflict. Something new is born of the conflict that doesn't in any way deny either of its aspects, but adds a third, utterly real entity, which in effect absorbs the tension.

†: The demands of the child within v. the demands of the present state, circumstances or the world.

* The penis, which 'produces' the child. *Playing with or beating the child :* * Masturbation.

Cripple ** Fear of impotence (§ CASTRATION).

Crowd ** Other people in general, public opinion, collective values. The dream may reveal the dreamer's attitude to the masses. * Nobody in particular, and therefore a disguise for the dreamer's own attitudes, possibly virulent – he put the crowd there, after all.

The crowd may be in the dream for the sole purpose of camouflaging one person in it who would otherwise stand out disconcertingly.

Many eyes on the dreamer : * Concern about appearances and the impression he makes in public. Or an inflated idea of his own importance.

'*Getting lost in the crowd*', *disappearing into it, and becoming one with it :* ** A desire not to be singled out, to avoid personal responsibilities and anxieties, to be hidden, secretive, anonymous.

** A crowd of thoughts, since one person may signify an idea. Again there may be a particular secret thought hidden in the crowd, which may then signify the mass of thoughts forever jostling in the unconscious.

One person pressing to the front : ** A main idea emerging from the confused mass of thoughts.

A swarm of people streaming by, a seething mass of people : * Violent emotions of the unconscious mind.

The Dreamer Dreams can reveal a lot of candid accurate information about how the dreamer really thinks of himself, but not what he's really like. However, what people think of themselves affects their lives considerably.

Dwarf (any grotesque gnomelike figure, imp or little man) ** The penis; and may indicate extreme pressure from the unconscious for the dreamer to recognize and come to terms with his sexual cravings and instincts.

In a woman's dream : * Her Animus (§ ARCHETYPES), the guardian of her unconscious mind, but with whatever limitation she associates with his mutilated outward form.

**An Emperor or Empress ** The parents, or other people of eminent importance to the dreamer. *Assassinating the emperor:* * The dreamer may be establishing his independence from his father (§ FAMILY).

A Film Star A glamorous public figure such as a film star will often correspond in various ways with the individual's dream man or dream woman, and therefore may feature in a man's dreams as his Anima and in a woman's dreams as her Animus (§ ARCHETYPES).

A young person dreaming of becoming a film star: May be an attempt to compensate for the conscious feeling of being plain and unnoticed.

Hero (any heroic figure)

In a man's dream: * The Self.

In a woman's dream: * The Animus (§ ARCHETYPES).

On a heroic quest, such as overcoming the monster, without slaying it: ** The conscious ego struggling with the forces of the unconscious.

There are many stories in which the hero kills the embodiment of all that is dark and spiteful, but in so doing he also kills the Wise Old Man (§ ARCHETYPES), indicating that his potential self is doomed never to reach maturity that way. He must find some other way to deal with his difficulties rather than obliterate them and thus also the vitality and energy that go with them.

If the hero dies and returns to life: * Rebirth, renewal, enlightenment.

Something insignificant may be his undoing: This weak point in one's inner being often arises from failure to concentrate on the fourth and least developed faculty of the mind (§) at the right time. Or possibly some other neglected aspect of the individual's character, of which the dream may be a forewarning.

†: *Hero/Villain:* Good v. evil. Megalomania v. self-sacrifice.

The heroic Self may appear in a young man's dreams or fantasies to lend him the confidence that he has this strength within him, perhaps in order to compensate for a weak father or to encourage him to stand on his own in rebellion against an oppressive father.

High priest, Astrologer, or anyone with similar esoteric knowledge * The Wise Old Man (§ ARCHETYPES).

Hitler The supreme example of irrational authority, he may figure in dreams as a code for a particularly difficult father, who may have given the individual a distorted view of all authority.

Important People ** The dreamer's parents, or somebody else of equal importance to the dreamer. Because of the highly subjective evaluations of dreams, people such as the current president or king and queen may be substituted for the parents in order to provide an image of the importance of the figures concerned; this avoids pointing directly at the parents, which might be disconcerting because of other contents in the dream.

An Inferior Figure (an inadequate person, whom the dreamer despises in the dream) ** The Shadow (§ ARCHETYPES). Each individual Ego will have its own complementary Shadow. For example, the person who prides himself on being modest and discreet may have a brash or flashy Shadow.

If this inferior side of oneself is totally ignored, it remains arrested and can never grow out of the particular feelings of inferiority that were structured by the family in childhood and may have become quite irrelevant since.

This figure may appear in dreams when it is time for the individual to reassess his own deficiencies, as they are now, not as they were. Otherwise the vague feeling of inferiority lurking at the back of his mind will continually break through to shatter his confidence just when he needs it.

The Intruder (a burglar, a tramp, a salesman, etc.) ** The Shadow. Or, in a woman's dream, her Animus (§ ARCHE-TYPES). *The dreamer invariably tries to keep him out, but once he does get in (after a change in the dreamer's conscious attitude), he usually turns out to be helpful in some later dream:* ****** There is something the dreamer needs to know, must recognize, usually about himself. With this new understanding, which seems suspect at first, comes the potential of maturity which may renew the individual's life.

In a young woman's dream, if the intruder assaults her : ** It is necessary for her to take the necessary next step in her relationships with men. In order to be adequately prepared for this she must mature and become independent.

In a married woman's dreams: * The need for a more satisfactory sexual relationship with her husband, for which she can usually make the necessary preparations; these will be the equivalent of leaving the door open rather than bolting and barring it.

Judge ** Somebody whose judgement concerns the dreamer, possibly his father, or God.

King ** The father. The father figure (§ ARCHETYPES), *especially if he is ancient or dying.* ** A dominant idea, a ruling or governing principle. What the dreamer considers majestic in himself or somebody else.

Ministers (including popes, bishops, etc.) * The Self as Wise Old Man.
In a woman's dream: * The Animus as father figure rather than lover.

Names of people Friends, acquaintances or anybody else known to the dreamer may be selected to play a part in the dream solely on account of their names. They may represent someone else with the same name, but are more significant in the dreamer's experience and more relevant in the context of the rest of the dream. Thus a child with a particular given name or surname may represent an old person who has either a given name or surname in common with the child. For example: *Someone in the dream who happens to be called Peter :* * Another Peter; or possibly a figure like St Peter guarding the gates of heaven, and therefore the individual's conscience. *Mary:* * Another Mary, or possibly the Virgin Mary, therefore the individual's notions about purity or whatever else he may associate with her.

Occasionally the name may convey a meaning: *Prentice:* * Apprentice, therefore learning. *Smith, Jones:* * Anybody. *Alexander:* * Alexander the Great, therefore greatness.

Trying to name spontaneously some unnamed person in a dream may help reveal who it really was or what he stood for in the dream.

Negro (or Red Indian) Whatever is different, other, strange. Repressed desires, taboo sexual practices. Often the Shadow (§ ARCHETYPES). Death (§ COLOURS, Black) or the Devil. People so fear their own instinctive cravings that they would always prefer to attack an external object (Jews, Negroes, etc.), futile though such a remedy obviously is.

Nun * The dreamer's 'sister'. * Somebody who is wanted by God, respected by other people; the idea of otherworldliness and purity.

Nurse * The dreamer's 'sister'.

Old People (the Wise Old Man, etc.) An old man who inspires awe, often a remote superior figure who is the image of fathomless wisdom and intuition; the embodiment of spiritual fatherhood; he may appear as prophet, philosopher, scientist, or beggar or the priest-king who is an intermediary between heaven and earth: ** The man's Self and the woman's Animus (§ ARCHETYPES). Universal fatherhood, and mankind's spiritual heritage. The meaning and order that lie deeper than the superficial chaos of life.
If small yet none the less powerful in governing the fate of the dreamer: * The Trickster, or black Magician (§ ARCHE-TYPES).
If he has lost an eye: * He has lost part of his insight, is only partially enlightened. *The hero may be charged with finding it.*
Several elderly men who may be disapproving: * The elders, the values of the past, tradition.
Older people: * Parents.
'The old man': * The dreamer's father.

A Wise Old Woman: the feminine equivalent of the Wise Old Man: ** The Great Mother: the woman's Self and a man's Anima (§ ARCHETYPES).

An old woman: * Somebody whom the dreamer considers to be behaving like an old woman. Dreams have a way of belittling a man by changing him into a woman.

Pirate * The plunderer and destroyer of the seas. Since the seas refer to the unconscious soul, whatever forces may be devastating that soul.

Police (Officials, occasionally a watchman) ** Control: Law and order – whether that of the universe as perceived by the individual's inner conscience, and therefore self-control, or such external authority as the individual's father or anyone who seeks to impose conventional morality, standard religious principles, etc. Therefore inhibitions. The conscious mind, which may be controlling or hindering the rest of the personality.

Calling in the police as protection: ** Appealing to the conscience for protection against one's impulses.

Masquerading as a policeman: * Trying to get official sanction for one's impulses.

†: *Police/criminal:* Conscience v. wayward impulses.

Prince and Princess ** The dreamer and his sister (the King and Queen often signify the parents). * The Hero and the Princess (§ ARCHETYPES).

If the dream is not recognized as belonging to a realm of its own, in which the individual is of supreme importance to himself (which is precisely what enables him to recognize and respect other individuals), and if this inner reality gets confused with the outside world, it may lead to a pseudo-self-importance, delusions of grandeur, etc.

Queen (not only a mythical queen, but often a queen now on the throne or an historical queen) * The individual's mother.

Servants * Servants of God, therefore priests, ministers and whatever the dreamer associates with these.

Maids: * The handmaids of the Lord.

Shopkeeper * The man with the scales of justice: conscience.

Soldiers * Obsessions.
Military discipline: ** Any other form of compulsion imposed by life; or inner coercion.
A soldier: * The Hero (§ ARCHETYPES). *If he is wounded:* * The individual's will and initiative are threatened. Unless it refers to castration and the fear of impotence (§ WOUNDS).

A Stranger
A shady individual, of the same sex as the dreamer, often standing slightly behind him; possibly a foreigner or a criminal: ** The Shadow (§ ARCHETYPES). Man confronts the greater part of himself as a stranger, and the stranger in a dream may indicate the first dark confused phase of getting to know this side of himself. *Fighting with a stranger:* ** Inner conflict with this figure.
* A strange aspect of someone else the dreamer knows. * The embodiment of all that is unknown, ambiguous, uncertain.
An awesome stranger: * The Self (§ ARCHETYPES). The individual may be estranged from his true Self.

Twins (including the double or mirror-image of a figure in the dream) ** Two sides of the same person, possibly the dreamer himself; an inner cleavage (§ NUMBERS, Two). * Someone else who is being 'two-faced'. The strife and deception between Esau and Jacob is typical of the struggle between twins.

The Unknown Man (who may take any form, from an imaginary youth, to some actual person whom the dreamer very much admires in life; he may be a rake or a hero, or the male equivalent of any aspect of the Unknown Woman)
In a woman's dream: ** The Animus (§ ARCHETYPES). The masculine force of intellect, independence, originality within.
In a man's dream: * The Self (§ ARCHETYPES).

The Unknown Woman (an imaginary sweetheart or heroine, but occasionally some actual girl barely known to

the dreamer but attractive; a priestess, a saint, a harlot, mistress, prima donna, a heroine or a seductress. Somebody unnamed but vaguely resembling a figure who is familiar to the dreamer)

In a man's dream: ** The Anima (§ ARCHETYPES). The feminine force within the man, the archetype of life.

The different images chosen by the unconscious to portray this archetype will be significant too, each with its different implications. One may be transformed into another during the course of the dream, indicating the various different qualities of the feminine force within the man. Her attributes, such as her pets, clothes, the objects around her, may reveal other aspects of her that may have been neglected by the dreamer.

PLACE The setting or background of the dream may refer to inner states of mind and particularly mood, or to a particular period in the dreamer's life associated with that place; or it may help identify the people with whom the dream is concerned. Occasionally a landscape reflects the contour of the body, especially the mother's body – mother earth.

Places quite unknown to the dreamer: Are particularly suitable settings for inner events, purely psychological situations and experiences, thoughts and feelings.

Unknown countryside that seems familiar: ** A constantly recurring situation in the dreamer's life, but each time it reappears it does so in a new guise.

A strange neighbourhood, possibly on the outskirts of a town: ** An unfamiliar part of the mind, on the outskirts, and therefore the unconscious.

Nocturnal landscapes: ** Excursions into the realm of the unconscious. Or a background impression of dark (§).

A dark overcast scene: * Depression, gloom.

A bright sunny place: * Gaiety, elation.

Cold, bleak or hostile places or serene friendly places: May all refer to the dreamer's general concept of the world.

In a series of dreams if the settings become lighter: ** An increase of conscious realization of the situation which inevitably alleviates it.

A secluded, sheltered place: ** Security, peace; a refuge.

A stuffy, oppressive place: ** The wish to get out, to become more extroverted perhaps. A previous refuge may become too confining in a later dream.

Wide-open spaces: ** Freedom; but also possible danger.

A barren place that the dreamer turns into a garden: ** An unpleasant aspect of himself that he could change; the potential of inner spiritual development.

Jungles: Are a suitable setting for thoughts about sexuality.

A fun fair or carnival: Could be trying to convey the idea that what is taking place in the dream is really quite fun. Thus an inhibited person dreamed of somebody making sexual advances at a fun fair.

Place frequently represents time-periods in the dreamer's life.

Landscapes: ** The layout of life, with the past lying behind and the future ahead. With mountainous difficulties, often self-imposed, to one side (§ MOUNTAINS) and green pastures of hopes that will be lushly fulfilled if the dreamer can get across the river (§ CROSSING).

Going back to a familiar, often beautiful, place: ** Childhood.

A lovely place: ** Youth; or the realm of fantasy.

An unfamiliar place: ** Memories to which the conscious waking mind has no access.

The particular memories associated with the place in the dream: ** A happy time, a miserable time, etc.

The place may be associated with particular people.

The place where the dreamer was born: ** His mother.

Places that don't seem quite right, that have been altered, are often composite scenes in which several places the dreamer knows have been lumped together: The various ingredients of the scene, once separated, may refer partly to mood or inner factors, while another part refers to a period of time when the dreamer was a certain age, and a third part points to a particular person who used to live there, etc.

The country where the dream takes place may have particular associations for the dreamer, or may have been included because of frequently encountered associations.

America: * Practical, materialistic race.

England : * Moral restraint; the stiff upper lip.

Egypt : * The fleshpots. But also ancient civilization and spiritual riches. And incest in the Royal Family.

Rome : * Unchained libido and brutality loose in the streets and arenas.

Turkey : * Polygamy.

PLANTS ** Growth: inner development. If the roots are neglected, the rest will wither.

PLAYING ** Masturbation – 'playing with oneself' – or 'sex play' in general. * Playing with ideas, which is often a necessary preliminary to serious activity.

For other sorts of playing, see Index.

The PLOT of the Dream Like plays, dreams are often naturally divided into episodes. If the individual recognizes these natural divisions, it may help him to understand the dream. Separating the various ingredients helps clarify what the dream is about:

The presentation : the characters taking part and the setting of the dream. In isolating these, the number of people and the different elements of the setting should be noted.

The complication : how the action begins.

The culmination : the result of each action – what becomes of it, what it leads to; thus establishing the relationship between cause and effect.

The conclusion (if any) : the dreamer may be left to draw his own conclusions from the dream, but sometimes it gives some partial indication of the solution to the problem, a new direction the dreamer might think about taking, etc.

PLOUGHING ** Intercourse. Fertility, fruitfulness.

The furrow : * The female genitalia – because of the obvious visual imagery and because planting refers to generation: reproduction, raising a crop, refers to raising children.

A ploughed field : * The Mother (§ ARCHETYPES).
An unploughed field : * A virgin. Or basic matter in contrast with the spirit.
Too old to plough : * Too old for intercourse.
** Some other task, often involving mental activity, from which the dreamer hopes to reap a harvest one day. The hard, thankless, heavy work is over: it remains only to put in the seed and wait.
To replough : * To go over the same ground again in the hope of rendering it suitable.

POISON The individual may have toyed with the fantasy of poisoning someone – perhaps in childhood – and though the idea has long been rejected and forgotten by the conscious mind, it is precisely this that has enabled it to crystallize among the patterns of the unconscious, making the individual feel guilty in a vague way. (The antidote for a poison is often the same substance as the poison, in dreams as in life.)

POLE (flag pole, fishing rod, truncheon, baseball bat, etc., especially with a light or flame on its end) *** The erect phallus; therefore sometimes refers to all that is masculine.

POSITION *** Moral standpoint; position in life.
Something in the wrong position : * Going about things in the wrong way. For example, a man dreamt that he walked in front of his plough and got cut to pieces by it.

Above/Below (upper, lower; up, down)
Anything higher, above – the upper part of the house, body, etc.: *** The dreamer's spirit and intellect. Everything in him that strives upward: his conscience, ideals, altruism. Heaven.
Anything underneath, below, downstairs: *** The sexual impulses. The base animal or sensual part of nature. The antisocial, immoral and anarchic. Earth. Just as the greatest development may be expected through recognition of all that

is inferior and rotten in one's character (§ SHADOW), so dreams often point to the necessity of going 'below' in order to broaden the individual's outlook so that he can avoid other, much greater pitfalls (hypocrisy, conceit, intolerance, etc.). The heights and depths of the personality balance each other as they are revealed together, and if this equilibrium is disturbed, the side that is being ignored may manifest itself in dreams. The roots must be in the ground: one part of the personality must be the firm deep foundation so that the other can soar into the sky. 'High stands on low' (Lao-tzu).

Upside down: ** Upheaval, as for instance when the spirit is made to serve base ends. Change. *'Turning everything upside down'* : May be necessary to find what one is looking for in order to reach the goal, the objective, which may be transformation.

Up and down: * The 'ups and downs' of some venture in life.

Back/Front ** The position of making love. *Thus, moving from a back to a front room:* Changing from homosexuality to heterosexuality.

Backward/Forward ** A regressive tendency, retreating into the past, in contrast with progress, moving ahead to meet the future.

The Centre (of a town, of a part of the countryside, of the world) (§ SHAPES, Centre.): ** The objective, the goal, the 'aim' as with a target. The dreamer may be recentring, finding his own real centre, which is the Self (§ ARCHETYPES).

Whatever holds the central position in the layout of the dream: ** What is the centre of attention. *If the 'I' of the dream is not central:* * The ego is no longer all-important.

Far/Near ** Time.

In the distance, a long way away: ** Remote in time, a long time ago.

Near: ** Recently, or 'near to the heart', 'near and dear'.

Opposite ** Opposing, and therefore a conflict with the person sitting opposite or whatever.

One thing placed opposite another: ** A contrary view. The significance of the object may indicate what this difference of opinion is about.

Changing the position of something, moving around to the opposite position, and in general putting things back to front or rearranging them: ** Another point of view which may be the direct opposite or just different.

Points of the Compass

The East: ** Where the sun rises; birth; conscious earthly life.

The South: ** Earthly warmth and passion.

The West: ** Sunset and death; the after-death state, which therefore implies a more spiritual orientation; rebirth: sunrise follows sunset.

The North: ** Darkness, the unknown; also more likely to be associated with the spirit.

†: *South/North:* ** Passions v. orderly directions of conscience.

The four cardinal points including four winds, etc.: ** The four faculties of the mind (§), intellect, emotion, intuition and sensation.

Right/Left *** Right and wrong; the correct and the incorrect, whether of the two sides of a person's or an animal's body, or two roads or ways to the left and right, or the object on the left contrasted with that on the right, or one side of the object such as the left barrel of a gun.

The right: *** Correct and moral behaviour. Those principles that have been accepted by society, such as marriage, heterosexuality, etc., and occasionally extroversion. ** The conscious active masculine principle.

The left: ** The sinister, the wrong, the instinctive. Anything vicious and immoral: criminal tendencies, incest, perversion. The feminine passive principle; sometimes the faculty of intuition.

Movement to the right: * The direction in which the sun moves, therefore something becoming conscious. *For example, a swastika with its arms moving clockwise from the centre* (卐): A Buddhist figure, it represents spiritual growth, awareness.

It was also the symbol used by the Nazi regime in Germany. *Whereas a swastika moving counterclockwise (卍) is in Tibet a sign of black magic; it represents the dark or sinister.*

Dreams will usually indicate the advantages of the right. But in the case of an overscrupulous, righteous or excessively idealistic person, they may point out something to the left that has been ignored and requires the dreamer's attention.

PREGNANT * Potential new life: anything full of possibilities, hopes.

PRISON ** Being restricted. One part of the personality may be restricting another; the conscious may be locking away the unconscious. In a man his masculinity may be keeping his emotions and the feminine side of his nature under lock and key. Or the restrictions may be imposed by the individual's conscience: he may be punishing himself for having violated his own code, or may express an unconscious wish that his impulses be kept under control.
The warden, the jailer: ** Conscience.
If the jailer ends up in his own prison: ** The danger of trying to limit the freedom of others is that you become limited and bound yourself.
** Society's attitudes may make the individual feel restricted, cornered, trapped, as in the case of one homosexual.

PROFESSIONS As with occupations (§), one may be substituted for another, and all will point to the professional type of man, and that particular aspect of his life.
Family doctor: * Father confessor.

Being PULLED ** A strong emotional attraction.
Someone pulling: ** Someone with a lot of influence: 'pull'.
A horse pulling well: ** The attraction is strong, but the identity of whoever is exerting it has been disguised (a stallion or a mare?).

PUNISHMENT ** The penalty the dreamer expects if he violates his conscience. 'Good people punish themselves in this way more than bad people' (Hall). This kind of self-punishment may be carried over into waking life – with plainly self-inflicted disappointments, etc. – in which case the person is often working out some similar atonement.

Being PUSHED ** Being 'pushed around', 'pushed about', pressured in some way. 'Being pushed for money'. Autoerotic pleasure: the pram, the swing.

RACE (whether the runners are animal or human) **
Rivalry (sometimes sexual rivalry between father and son or mother and daughter).

RAIN ** Being refreshed. Being delivered from an arid period, emotional or intellectual. * Urine, therefore semen.

RELIGIOUS IMAGERY By discarding the stale conventional forms and using vivid and often startling images, dreams can often reintroduce the individual to fundamental 'truths' that may be vital to his welfare, but that he is neglecting.

There are two ways of neglecting the underlying reality that is essential for salvation or essential to deeper wisdom, profounder understanding, growth rather than atrophy at a certain point in life. The first is to accept the superficial and communal aspect of religion and never explore beyond it to the truth itself of which the rituals and so on were only outward signs. The other is a prolonged reaction against the outward form of religion that also denies access to the inner meaning. Dreams may try to jolt the individual into respecting the needs of his inner spirit.

Like other factors in the mind, spirituality struggles for existence; if it is in too much danger of being neglected, it will appear in dreams in a way likely to have the greatest impact on the individual: in its negative and most horrifying form. This is why those who have most denigrated spiritual values appear to think that religious belief is founded on nightmares.

Only the human spirit can recognize its own limitations and so transcend them, relating to what-is-so even though we don't know it, instead of assuming that what we don't know doesn't exist. Only the spirit can grow in accord with the essential nature of things and their unknown Source.

†: The spirit v. the world or the flesh. True to their usual function, dreams try to keep a balance between inner spiritual values and sexuality, worldliness, life. Those who make an enemy of the spirit, either by neglecting it or by only accepting its outward form, will have this brought to their attention. Those who are in danger of making an enemy of life, by concentrating too exclusively on the spirit, are likely to have dreams that attempt to compensate for this – especially where the individual spurns the world and his instincts, more out of fear of them than of love of the spirit. The instincts, as the source of passion and enchantment, must never become desiccated but rather be transformed in relation to the individual's ideals and aspirations.

Ostensibly religious dreams may in fact have nothing to do with religion.

God : * Somebody the dreamer worships, idolizes.
Old and New Testaments : * A will, an inheritance.
Priest/Prophet : * The past v. the future.

Angel ** Freedom, pure being. The unearthly, and therefore detachment from women.
†: Freedom v. Security.
Dark, fallen angels : ** Homosexuality.
Angels of warning : * What the dreamer should avoid, which way not to go, etc. (§ FLYING).

Buddha ** Someone who renounced home life to seek and fulfil his own destiny. May have a significance similar to Christ.

Christ ** The perfect man; through whom the individual can find the immortal within himself. Also the reconciliation between God and man, and therefore between the spirit and the flesh. *If depicted as having suffered :* ** Redemption through suffering: the selfish and demanding ego yields voluntarily to the sacrifice, dies and is reborn as the individual's true Self (§ ARCHETYPES). The dream may indicate that the individual is refusing or neglecting to integrate this ideal into his life.

Church § BUILDINGS.

Church Music * The Christian spirit.

Devil (Hell, etc.) ** The sexual drives; repressed unconscious or instinctive life; the abyss of impassioned dissolution. The Shadow or Black Magician (§ ARCHETYPES). The father, who is a rival to the adolescent for the mother's affection. Dread arising from infantile experiences of fear.

The Devil may feature in dreams when the individual is thinking of abandoning his inherited standards in favour of something chosen for himself, which is often more self-indulgent and challenges him to reassess his principles. In this sense the Devil can be seen as the servant of God, in that he punishes sin.
Hell: § FIRE.

Ghosts (spirits, etc.) ** Autonomous forces within, independent of the individual's will. Often the Anima or Animus (§ ARCHETYPES).

God When the image of God, which exists in the mind, appears in dreams, it may point to the individual's need to realize his fullest possible inner potential in order to undergo that most profound and powerful experience, which man has called 'God'. This encounter between the human and the Divine, by means of symbols that point beyond themselves, all but destroys the ego in an experience resembling death. Returning from the depths of utter extinction, he will be at one with the indestructible matter and the enduring spirit of which he is a part.

Mary, the Mother of God ** The Great Mother (§ ARCHE-TYPES). Mother Earth, but also the seat of Wisdom. Mary symbolizes matter itself, transformed through many stages of life, through many phases of evolution, from generation to generation, in preparation for its encounter with the Spirit.

A Religious Service * Moral redemption.
Being too shabby for church: * Being beyond such redemption.
Religious experiences may be expressed in more pagan or mythical settings, or take the form most likely to impress the individual.

RESCUING ** Making contact with the other person and leaving him or her indebted to you. Therefore the desire to be loved by that person, and possibly to have intercourse with him or her. (Consider the number of people in fiction who fall in love with their rescuers.)
Rescuing the young maiden from the dragon, etc.: ** Rescuing the mother from the clutches of the father in order to have her for oneself. Or the individual may be rescued (by the powers of womanhood?) from some figure or image representing homosexuality.
* Saving souls, or saving the situation in a way that may refer to ambition or power.
Attempts at rescue may be a camouflage to exonerate the dreamer for having put the other characters in such a hazardous plight (§ ACTION OF THE DREAM).

RIDING (whether a horse, animal, bicycle, motorbike, etc.) ** Erotic attachment to whoever or whatever is represented by the thing ridden. Passion. Mastery. Conquest, usually in love. Riding is an image of intercourse and almost invariably has strong sexual associations. The unconscious object of erotic fantasies may be disclosed in such a dream, even though disguised in images. The conscious directing of primitive energy and unconscious forces, symbolized by the animal, motorbike, etc., thus rendering that energy fruitful or useful.
'Being ridden': * 'Being hag-ridden', being possessed, owned, guided, sometimes by the devouring and destructive aspect of the mother (§ ARCHETYPES, the Terrible Mother).

The harness: ** The will: conscious control.

'Unbridled': ** Passion that is out of control.

In a heterosexual's dream, whatever is ridden: ** Somebody of the opposite sex.

In a man's dream, failing to manage the horse, etc., or being thrown or kicked: ** Fear of women arising from an inability to master them.

A horse that has never been ridden: ** A virgin.

Holding the reins tightly: ** Keeping tight control; but if they are held too tightly, this could anger the horse and so make it unmanageable.

The reins slipping from the hands: * A time in the past when the dreamer actually lost control.

Riding down people on foot: * Sadistic tendencies (§ JOURNEYS, Cars running down pedestrians).

ROOTED (to the spot) § PARALYSED.

ROPES ** Umbilical cord: attachment to the mother. * Penis.

SACRIFICES *There may be a sacrificial altar or it may just be a question of killing and cooking an animal ritualistically:* *** Any form of self-sacrifice the dreamer is contemplating or hoping to evade. It could be the sacrifice of his animal instincts, his freedom, his individuality, and could be on behalf of his parents, his wife, his children or for the sake of his religion.

There is usually some expectation of spiritual power and energy attached to any form of sacrifice, but especially when egotistic, self-interested aims are abandoned in favour of following whatever forces are at work in a particular person's life, and in the universe in general – apart from the relief of no longer being pitted against those forces, which were too powerful. So ** yielding to life's demands, submitting to life-as-it-is, rather than insisting on personal satisfaction.

Sacrifice of an animal: ** Fleshly instincts being transmuted into spiritual power. To be human and to know God requires the willing sacrifice of the licentious indulgence of animal instinct, in return for spiritual benefits.

The willingness of the creature sacrificed: ** Instinct is ready and wants to be transformed into spirit.

Sacrifice of something black: * Sacrifice to the gods of the underworld.

Sacrificing the hare: Has much the same significance as the sacrificial Lamb of Christianity and is especially associated with Easter and rebirth. This is emphasized if white comes into the dream (white plates, dishes, moon, snow); if the hare is simply killed and cooked, this may amount to sacrifice.

†: Taking v. giving, having v. being, merit v. grace.

SALT ** The essence, the essential inner being, the soul; 'the salt of the earth', 'if the salt loses its savour'. The incorruptible, the eternal; things are pickled in brine to preserve them. And therefore the higher insight and spiritual wisdom that come from seeing things in the light of eternity. White (§ COLOURS). Sometimes semen and fertility.

SCHOOL *** The earliest experience of social convention and restriction, which has so great an emotional impact that it is never forgotten by the unconscious and is often used in dreams to show up the current conflict with its equivalent triumphs and humiliations.

The incident in school, once related to the present circumstances, should reveal the individual's underlying life conflict. School, with its grades, uniforms, reprimands, and so on that seem all-important at the time, is like a microcosm of later life, which in turn, if seen from a wider perspective, isn't so desperately important either. This may be what the dream is trying to say through a comparison of present circumstances with events at school.
* Other events during the period of adolescence: habits the dreamer has failed to outgrow, therefore arrestedness, failure to mature and forget about the past; possibly homosexuality (§ SEX).
* Discipline, therefore self-discipline, self-control. The intellectual masculine principle, as it modifies nature.

SEARCHING The dreamer may already know what he's looking for and is only pretending not to be able to find it (§ NEGATIVES, in Dreams) because he doesn't like the consequences or implications of whatever is signified.

The SEASONS
Spring: ** Childhood.
Summer: ** Youth: the flower of life.
Autumn: ** Manhood, maturity: when the individual's life should bear fruit.

Winter : ** Old age, sterility.
In a series of dreams, the summer that follows winter : * Convictions about life after death (§ SUN).

The SENSES * The four qualities of mind (§):
Sight : * Intellect.
Smell : * Intuition.
Hearing : * Emotion.
Taste, touch : * Sensation.

SEWING ** Coitus, because of the way the needle penetrates the material. Masturbation, because the gesture is similar.

SEX Dreams reveal the whole range of man's inner sexuality, comparatively free of social strictures. The more somebody tries to ignore his own sexual nature, and fails to give due reverence to this life impulse within him during his waking hours, the more likely he is to see it displayed before him in his sleep – unless he manages to suppress his dreams too.

Dreams restore a balance, especially where a life has been overintellectualized or idealized, in which case dreams may become increasingly vivid until they burst into life, perhaps forcing a person to make contact with other people and thus open the path to his emotions.

Sexuality is the most obvious visual image of intense love, and since dreams express themselves visually for the most part, it is the means they use to represent a longing for closeness and union with another person; or even the yearning to be united – at one – with all that lies outside the ego. Whitmont suggests that to relate to sexuality as if it were a vivid personal experience of the powers-that-be, of the reality that is beyond conscious willing, is enough to turn a perversion into a source of new life. Meaningful in itself, it also leads to the unfathomable qualities of love, procreation and Divine energy. And we have paid for our lack of reverence by an arid inability to relate to our own instincts and feelings.

Bisexuality The dreamer often and easily identifies with the other sex: this may indicate an inner cleavage and conflict between the masculine and feminine potentials within the personality; or that the Animus or Anima is demanding attention (§ ARCHETYPES).

Emission An emission during a dream indicates the sexual nature of the whole dream, however obscure and unlikely the images of the dream are. An orgasm cannot lie. A dream culminating in an emission may reveal the object of the dreamer's desire as well as his inner conflict. The images in the dream will reveal the dreamer's attitude to sex: he may see it as something mechanical, which can be turned on and off (a water tap), or as something dangerous (a wild beast), or as something wicked, depraved, dirty, etc.

Fetishes Freud saw all fetishes as an unconscious inducement to asceticism, which implies that man doesn't become a celibate to avoid the repercussions of his sexual inclinations, but at an unconscious level cultivates certain tendencies in order to pursue a life of celibacy, unmolested. This design could of course go wrong later (§ SEX, Perversion).

Hermaphrodite * The union of opposites. The two opposite poles within the psyche, in this case the masculine and the feminine, cause a tension that amounts to intense creative activity within. The two finally become one only in a third, which is the equivalent of their offspring; thus neither loses its individual nature. The hermaphrodite may be the healing symbol for accepting the latent masculinity or femininity.

Homosexuality When the ego seems unable to realize its own virility, it searches for it in the outside world. The homosexual disguises himself psychically as a girl, in order not to reveal his erroneously assumed lack of masculinity in a heterosexual love. By opting for the feminine aspect of himself, a homosexual may be inclined to repress the masculine in himself which may lead to a feeling of deficiency and emptiness later in life. This would be the time to cultivate this other frustrated side – within himself, not necessarily by affairs with women; not any more than a heterosexual individual needs to have affairs with men in order to cultivate his Anima or the feminine in him (§ ARCHETYPES, Anima).

In the inner sphere homosexuality indicates a striving for union with all that is masculine and that for some reason has been experienced too little or not at all. Hence dominant mothers and weak or absent fathers are often the cause.

Although undoubtedly the individual will only feel secure enough to confront the opposite sex without fear of being engulfed once he has first established his essential masculinity, projecting this inner deficiency on to another man and hoping to make up for it by physical contact with him is none the less primitive (§ SEX, Semen) and often not very effective. The problem is inward and of the mind, so it is there that the solution can be found.

* The repression of heterosexuality, originally because of the fear of incest, as a substitute for incest.
* 'The psychic bond between men which is one of the foundations of society' (Layard).

'Flashes of homosexual desire may be found in the dreams of anyone' (Gutheil), and may refer to any of the various underlying aspects of the problem that always exist in a latent form, but matter only in so far as they cause distress below the surface; this could be manifested, for example, in too much determination to demonstrate one's masculinity by being promiscuous or unfaithful.

If the dreamer plays the masculine role: * Victory over a rival.

Dream interpretation, like any other form of deciphering, is often a question of gradually filling in gaps. After a bit of experience with one's own dreams it becomes possible to conjecture (for example) that if a man dreams of playing the feminine role in a homosexual relationship, this has much in common with dreams of castration (§).

Although it is regretted that the material in this section treats more of the underlying meaning of homosexuality in men's dreams, much of it could also be adapted – with caution – by a woman, as long as this is done in relation to particular dreams, and so that she can recognize the validity and significance of such speculations for herself.

Incest ** The desire for love.

In a man's dream: * The desire to re-enter the primordial unconscious state of being one with the whole of nature. Thus, a striving after immortality, as well as the regressive desire to be free from responsibilities by re-entering the womb.

In a woman's dream: Indicates the 'desire for love' (§ FAMILY).

It would be false to conclude that dreams of incest indicate a desire for actual incest. Spiritual and psychological phenomena put into concrete pictorial images are never to be confused with biological fact.

Intercourse (or extreme physical embraces): ** The wish for love.

The other partner may represent an idea; for example, a man dreamed of making love to a woman who led a very active life: * The wish that his own wife should play a less passive role in life as well as in their sexual relations. That he may also have desired the other woman was relatively unimportant.

If a child is born of the union in the dream: * The 'conjunction' of the inner alchemy from which the Self emerges whole.

Being interrupted while attempting intercourse: ** Inhibitions. The unforeseen event or person who interrupts may indicate why the individual is reluctant (§ FAMILY).

Being clothed while making love: * An attempt to cover one's shame; therefore guilt.

If the female genitalia cause anxiety: * An unconscious memory of the shock of being born.

Rape: * The dreamer is unready for sexual relations with that person.

Kiss * Fertility (§ KILLING).

Perversion ** An attempt on the part of the unconscious to evade the all-important issue of love, so fraught with high expectations and possible disappointments. Dreams, sexual fantasies, and a sex life that is an expression of these fantasies all have much in common; they will complement and compensate for the dominant waking attitude, especially where this is exaggeratedly one-sided. For example:

Sadism: ** The individual behaves much too timidly, so that this has become the only outlet for his aggressive and protective instinct, the impulse of self-preservation and survival.

Masochism or infantilism: ** Being so dominant, mature and responsible in waking life that the unconscious seeks to compensate this with the longing to be controlled, given no choice, helpless. Also ** repressed sadism.

Sadism, masochism and all the other ingredients of sexuality exist in everyone in latent form and sometimes express themselves in dreams. The dreamer will usually employ some other figure to act on his behalf in order to avoid responsibility – possibly one of the ancient divinities who is half-man and half-beast (§ SEX, Fetish).

Phallus ** The life impulse. All that is active, vital, creative.

A galaxy of phalli and phallic images appearing continually in dreams: The individual is either ignoring sexuality in waking life or is consciously devaluing it. Jung cites Freud's bias towards seeing sexuality as the chief content of the unconscious as a typical example of this, and claims that it arose from Freud's under-valuation of sexuality

A woman with a phallus, in a man's dream: ** The feminine within the dreamer: his Anima (§ ARCHETYPES). Or he feels effeminate, feels like a woman inside although equipped with a penis. ** He thinks of that person as too masculine, and therefore possibly threatening his own masculinity. ** An inner cleavage between heterosexuality and homosexuality (§ SEX, Bisexuality, Homosexuality).

A wooden phallus: May emphasize that the dream is not about the flesh but about the equivalent life force and creative power of the spirit.

Semen ** The sign of masculinity; it has been used by primitive tribes to anoint the male youth in a form of initiation which replaces the female influence with the male. Similarly, homosexuality is not only pleasurable and meaningful in itself; it is also a sign of passing on all that is masculine to the youth and thereby increasing, not diminishing, his physical virility as well as his masculine qualities of mind.

Dreams are also primitive and may reflect such practices

and rites, as if vestiges of them still existed in the unconscious mind. Both the rituals and the dreams may have had their source in the unconscious, which has its own standards of behaviour.

Venereal Disease * A diseased relationship, and therefore an incestuous relationship.

Geometrical SHAPES (patterns, etc.) ** The fundamental structures of a man's nature. The basic shape his life is taking. Beyond the sphere where ideas take on animal or human form, dreams have frequently revealed a more abstract realm of shapes, with a radiant presence, that are akin to deities. These shapes are plainly nothing in themselves; but that they have considerable symbolic significance has been demonstrated (the cross, the swastika, the crescent). In dreams they are usually a reconciling symbol that indicates that the individual is beginning to rise above adversity by accepting the nature of things-as-they-are. In its wake the acceptance brings serenity, peace.

The number of sides the shape has will be significant: § NUMBERS. And they will usually be coloured: § COLOURS.

Even if the shapes are not abstract and luminous, the shape of concrete objects in a dream may still have some of the same significance, though not as powerfully.

The Centre ** The inner core of man, as well as the hub of the universe, the eternal source of energy. The ungodly walk around the edge of the circle without ever reaching the centre (§ POSITION, Centre).

Circle ** The inner being. The Self (§ ARCHETYPES). The cycle of human life within the uninterrupted flow of eternity. Undifferentiated wholeness: unity and perfection, but not in any narrow limited sense. Life moves in cycles, and the eternal principle of the universe has often been represented as the complete circle. This includes the movement from non-ego in the womb, through ego, and back to non-ego again. 'The soul according to tradition has a round form' (Jung).

A circular object such as a bowl of fruit or a sphere with eyes: May have the same significance as the circle: that which is orderly and complete in itself, with everything necessary for its own existence. ** The female genitalia, therefore a woman, often the Mother (§ ARCHETYPES).

A circle with a dot in the centre: ** A woman.

A black circle or sphere: ** A black sun (§), hence the extinction of active intelligence that is madness (§ SHAPES, Mandala).

Crescent (including sickle and crescent moon) ** The rising power of the feminine; all that is emotional, mysterious and irrational. In the right circumstances, when the individual's life has been starved of emotional content, may bring about renewal as the mystery is revealed more fully.

Cross *The four arms pointing in opposite directions:* ** The nature of life is to be torn apart by conflict, torment, suffering, and through this to reach perfection. Meanwhile opposing drives force us in different directions at once, nailed to the tree of life.

The intersection: * The possibility of the union of opposites.

The three upper arms: * The Trinity.

The fourth, plunged into the ground: * Base matter, the underworld, and the forces of darkness and evil.

Lines A straight line: ** The ego.

Two lines, including railway lines: ** The principle of duality and conflict. A life determined for the most part by circumstances because the free will is too weak to affect it; living mechanically (§ NUMBERS, One, Two).

The Mandala *The word 'mandala' means circle, but it can also be applied to all the significant shapes that occur in dreams or present themselves spontaneously to the conscious mind, first appearing as an unimpressive dot or point. Often there is a square within the circle, or vice versa, which may appear in the dream in the form of gardens: a square garden with a round pool in it, a square island in a round pool, rose gardens or rose-windows, elaborated flowers, castles, cities, courtyards, if laid out* *in circular or quadratic form. Mandalas may also take the form of an eye, with an iris and pupil, or be egg-shaped or spiral; or they may appear as colourful patterns in material, mosaics, etc.:* ** The basic order and layout of the mind as a whole: the structure of the Self is the principle of order and meaning as against chaos; may express religious or philosophical ideas in pictorial terms, and expresses the essence of the individual's particular attitude towards his Self. The forces that bind the whole character into a unity in spite of the inner tensions that seem to be tearing it apart at times, and mandalas have symbolic power to protect the individual from inner disruption or even from outside forces that threaten his essential nature. In this sense the mandala represents rebirth into a spiritual realm, a central inner space (like the square keep of the castle) where adverse circumstances can no longer touch you.

The mandala is the vessel of transformation that binds and subdues the lawless powers belonging to the world of darkness, which will also be represented by dark shapes inside and outside the circle. It expresses the need for order which it also supplies, symbolically.

The fundamental shapes of matter, the undifferentiated and chaotic elements in the individual's life may all be represented. For example, wild animals may roam parts of the garden.

The circumference of the circle, the edge of the mandala: ** The protective skin around the individual, like the bark around a cross-section of tree.

In a series of mandala dreams: The individual may observe his striving towards balance, wholeness.

The colours (§). Should gradually become brighter as the individual strives towards inner development.

Ultimately there may be some symbolic representation of the identification of individual being with Supreme Being. The mandala then becomes a window opening on to eternity. The mandala of a dream will become more effective if drawn and coloured in. It is much easier to note it down visually rather than verbally. Being able to draw well doesn't matter and is sometimes even a disadvantage, if it inhibits the spontaneous free expression of the diagram, which should be allowed to take directions of its own in being put down. A series of such drawings over a period of time, stemming from one original dream, may reflect the path of inner development.

The mandala of dreams is distinguished from the Buddhist Wheel of Fortune or World Wheel, which refers to the temporal sphere rather than the inner realm.

Patterns (in cloth, mosaic, etc.) ** The pattern of life. The pattern may be complex but harmonious, or just plain chaotic.

The contrasts in colours and so on: * The conflicts. As with the mandala, the individual may be able to complete the grandiose pattern with his own individual piece.

Spiral ** The primary processes of the id. Evolution.

If the spiral is towards the centre: It nevertheless gets there by an indirect route.

A clockwise spiral, moving outward to the right: * A movement towards consciousness; *if counterclockwise:* * Movement towards the unconscious, probably regressive.

Any fluid movement of lines within one of the shapes, whether inclining to the left or right, may have this significance (§ POSITION, Right/left).

Square or Cube ** Quaternity: to the trinity of being, consciousness and love is added a fourth element: matter – the inner potential becomes material, actual in time and space. Especially if the square is in any way related to a triangle earlier in the dream, or in former dreams.

A square within a circle: ** The latent possibility of unity and order: the process of becoming, begetting. The inner being may give birth to something concrete. The 'straight, upright', sincere and 'well-regulated' life. Also, standing 'foursquare' to face all in a way that often subdues and reconciles conflicting elements.

The figure within a square or quadratic space: ** The Self, whole. The Wise Old Man (in a man's dream) or the Great Mother (in a woman's dream). *A square table, courtyard, etc., may have this significance* (§ NUMBERS, Four).

Star ** Destiny. Whatever gives a man's life its direction and guides him towards his inner goal: 'follow your star'.

A bright star : * Artistic, intellectual or mystical achievement.
Falling stars : * Failing hopes, disastrous changes, whether within the mind or in social affairs.

The five-pointed star : ** A shape that evokes the fundamental structure of living matter, therefore the material bodily man with the thinking, emotional, motive, instinctive and sexual aspects all in harmony. If the individual concentrates on one aspect of his being and neglects others, he inevitably gets stuck at a certain stage and cannot mature any further.

The six-pointed star, which is made up of one triangle pointing upward and another pointing downward : ** The reconciliation of the physical and the spiritual, the outside world and the inner realm; the wisdom that arises from this union of opposites, that brings a man to the knowledge of objective reality, beyond the sphere of everyday shocks, disappointments, etc. (§ NUMBERS, Five, Six).

Swastika *With its arms moving clockwise :* * The ideal man; *moving counterclockwise :* * The sinister (§ POSITION, Right/left).

Triangle (including huts, pyramids, etc.) ** The trinity, which within the individual is his being, his consciousness and his love. The spiritual and the eternal aspect of man, and the potential that has yet to be realized.

The triangle as half of the six-pointed star : * A lack of balance. *If the triangle points upward :* Too much emphasis on the upper realm; vice versa if the triangle points downward (§ POSITION, Above/below). Or because the triangle is associated with the number 3 (§ NUMBERS, Three): ** Male genitals, and the sexual sphere.

There is a game based on shapes in which you draw a square, a circle and a triangle, and then get someone else to elaborate each of the basic shapes into a drawing. Whatever he makes of the square is supposed to relate to his outlook on the world, the circle to his inner being, and the triangle to his or her sex life.

SHOOTING ** Assaulting someone sexually. (§ WEAPONS, AGGRESSION).

SILENCE * The still, dark silence of death.

SIZE *Things being very small, doll-sized or actually shrinking in size during the dream:* ** Dwindling in perspective because they are far away now – that is, they happened a long time ago, probably in childhood. (§ POSITION, Far/near). Alternatively, *if things are extra large:* ** Childhood, because things as seen through the eyes of a child did seem big, and dreams recapture this impression by making them proportionately bigger.

A giant or big man: ** The father.

The ledge of a mountain: ** The mother's bosom. Things seeming large may be related to the fact that the ego is now feeling small and as defenceless as a child. Dreams may make something big, in order to emphasize its importance.

Anything that grows big in the hand, for example a key: ** The penis.

The little man who conquers all, or something very small but very powerful: * The spirit, the Self (§ ARCHETYPES).

Larger/smaller, animal, etc.: * The male/the female.

SKY ** The heavens.

Blue skies: ** Aimless evasions; creative potential that hasn't been realized.

Something powerful descending from the sky, such as a huge hand, an air raid, a storm (§), or a shape (§) as a symbol of truth: ** The intervention of God in the affairs of the dreamer, wreaking destruction or coming to his aid.

SLEEP ** Death. * Some part of the dreamer, such as his conscience or his faith, is asleep.

SNOW ** The emotionally cold, frigid.

Someone standing in the snow: ** Someone who has acted callously towards the dreamer.

Snow-capped peaks: ** Solitude, introversion, the 'winter of the soul', suffering – but suffering that in fact protects the ground and the roots (of being) from the even severer frosts. * Winter sports; holidays, rest, recuperation. * Whiteness (§ COLOURS, White). Purity, innocence or direct intuitive knowledge. White linen. *An expedition into the snow:* * An expedition into the white sheets of somebody's bed.

SPECTACLES ** Clearsightedness.
A contrast between the two lenses: * A conflict in outlook.

STAR * A spark of Divine truth (§ SHAPES, Star).

STATUES ** Somebody who has been 'put on a pedestal', 'idolized'; or some institution, such as the dreamer's religion, that he has worshipped in rather a dead, awestruck manner.
The image has become tarnished, defaced or is deformed in some way: ** The person (often the mother) or the institution no longer seems so wonderful to the dreamer.
A figure being chiselled or moulded: ** The dreamer himself being 'shaped' or 'moulded' by someone else. *If by a female figure:* * His mother and her influence in forming his character.
People turned to stone, figures that still move but are made of stone: 'Petrifaction', stultification (§ STONES).
   The statue may be commemorating the dead (a tombstone) and could refer to death; if it relates to someone still living, possibly to death wishes. *A monument to someone who is actually dead:* * A wish to keep his memory alive.
Statues (or objects) coming alive: ** New potentialities awakening in the dreamer. New life within the dreamer is being projected on to outside objects. Such dreams often accompany falling in love, when certain emotions well up for the first time and seem to open up new worlds. *A religious statue coming to life:* ** What was a dead theoretical concept suddenly has new inner meaning for the dreamer. *If the statue that comes to life is full of rage, fury:* * The potential resentment and anger within the dreamer may break out with disastrous effects, if he doesn't do something about it in time.

STIFF *The dreamer's body being stiff:* ** Inner rigid attitudes that could be to compensate for a lack of constancy in everyday life. ** The rigidity of old age, and thoughts of death. ** 'Stiffening' with horror.

STONES ** Inner sterility. *Live objects turned to stone:* ** What was once living youthful experience is now only a dead memory, associated with heaviness and depression. (This can happen after a longish period of perfect harmony that has become so limiting that it is a dead end.)
People or even whole towns turned to stone: ** Emotional sterility, probably on the part of the dreamer, who as a result cannot relate to other people who seem 'unmoved' by his plight, immovable, greet him with 'stony' silence, who seem robbed of life and warmth simply because he feels nothing for them. The dreamer should now concentrate on the emotional side of his life (§ MIND).
Being hit with stones: * Being stoned, in punishment.
Beautiful or especially precious stones: * The indestructible Self (§ JEWELS).
Rocks: * The earthy. The Mother (§ ARCHETYPES).

STORMS ** Outbursts of emotion, desire or instinct. Extreme mental agitation. The difficulties encountered in life.
Violent storms: ** Violent passions, 'storms' of emotion.
If the dreamer's spouse appears in the dream: ** The 'stormy' aspect of their marriage.

Lightning ** The Spirit, the divine will striking the dark substance of nature. The life force.
Flashes of lightning: * 'Flashes' of awareness, intuition or revelation. These may occasionally bring disaster, as with the sudden realization that one's partner has been unfaithful. *If the lightning transfigures the body of someone who might represent the dreamer:* * The animal being transformed into the spiritual, the bestial into the celestial. A sudden unexpected and overpowering change within. The glimpse of enlightenment and freedom: the divine birth of light in the soul 'which lasteth a flash'.

Although intuition is often the neglected inferior function of the mind, which therefore remains the most spontaneous and 'stormy', usually operating in 'flashes', if any of the other three faculties is equally neglected it could operate in the same spasmodic way, and the lightning could refer to that.

Thunder * A fart.

Dreams of SUCCESS ** An attempt to compensate for failure and insignificance in waking life.

SUCKING * Draining of resources, whether emotional or material: 'sucking dry'. * Being sycophantic: 'sucking up'. * Babyhood.

SUN ** The light of consciousness. Intellect, active intelligence.

A scorching sun: * An excess of intellectuality, making the character 'dry, arid', as the sun scorches the desert. Concentrating more on the unconscious and the emotions would correct the balance. (In hot climates where the sun is a threat or a menace it will more often be a symbol of that menace; in temperate climates it more often signifies creative energy, fruitfulness, etc.).

Sunrise: ** The dawn of consciousness, new realizations: it 'dawned' on him. Also, new beginnings: youth, hope. Potential progress and growth, especially towards maturity.

Noon, midday: * Manhood.

Sunset, plunging towards darkness: ** The decline of creative energy, especially in old age.

The black sun: ** Madness or death, but in any event the death of active intelligence. Possibly profound depression.

In a series of dreams, which may have been filled with images of old age and death, if the sun rises again in rejuvenated splendour: * The Life itself that is eternal and in which we share. Or the strength of the dreamer's convictions that see him through some 'dark period' to another 'sunrise'. The sun is not only an image of this life force; it may also be personified in dreams as a sun hero or sun god, and play some similar role.

** The Father, or the Self, the Wise Old Man (§ ARCHE-TYPES). * The phallus.
Sunset leading to sunrise, the sun sinking into the sea or the earth (that is, the Mother) from which the new sun is born the following day: Spiritual rebirth.
Sun: * 'Son'.

Or, rarely, and usually in a woman's dream: * The feminine principle, the Great Mother, the Self (§ ARCHETYPES).

Artemidorus considered that to see the sun in a dream is good, 'except for those who want to keep something secret or hid'. And more recently Stekel mentions someone whose dread of sunlight was involved with his dread of a truth becoming known.

SURGERY (operations, etc.) * Interference with the individual's way of life, his thoughts, his values. Wounds (§). Sacrifice (§).
Anaesthetic: Renders the sacrifice worthless.
The doctors: * Other authorities.

Being SUSPENDED ** The embryo phase of life.
†: Progressive v. regressive tendencies.

SWINGING (rocking, etc.) ** The to-and-fro motion of the cradle, the idyllic existence of babies; or the same motion on the swings in childhood. The womb, the happiness of childhood, possibly in contrast with present difficulties. * Churchbells, marriage, religion.

TEETH § BODY, Teeth.

TELEPHONING ** Contacting, getting in touch; therefore touching and even intercourse. Making contact with the unconscious.
Being cut off: ** Death; the dream may throw light on the individual's attitude to it.

TIME Dreams seldom have chronological sequence: whatever is significant or relevant to the emotional content of the dream, or the train of thought, forms the link between one scene and another. Thoughts about the dreamer's whole past and future may be telescoped into one dream. Years, days and hours are undifferentiated: one may stand for another. For example an image like teeth falling out (§ BODY, Teeth) may express the emotional upheaval of growing up (past) and growing old (future).

Time of Day ** The dreamer's age. * Other dates that are significant to him. The unconscious has its own accurate calendar whose dates were significant even though the dreamer's conscious mind has forgotten about them long ago. Once unearthed, these often reveal the cause of otherwise unaccountable depressions and so on.
A day: ** A lifetime.
Morning: ** Youth.
Afternoon: ** Manhood, womanhood.
Evening: ** Old age. May refer to a time for casting off daytime attitudes and preparing for the coming 'night'(death).
Particular hours of the day: ** A particular age. Thus *10:30:*

** Ten and a half years old, and so refers to some significant event when the dreamer was that age (§ NUMBERS). *11 :00:* 'The eleventh hour', the last moment perhaps to make some necessary changes in order to find fulfilment. And it may be just past or just before eleven o'clock. *It's late, being late for trains, etc.:* ** The desire for more time, the longing to be younger, etc.

Any reference to eternity: * Death.

Any reference to history, including historical costumes, settings: ** The past; the dreamer's own past, often his childhood.

Anything prehistoric: * Prenatal experiences, traces of which may be retained in the unconscious.

Just as time may refer to age, so a certain number of days: ** That number of years.

Three days: * The period between Good Friday and the resurrection, and therefore to a similar process of rebirth taking place within the individual's being.

Watching the hands of a clock move: * 'Going round in circles', therefore inner tension.

Age

Someone else of a certain age in the dream: ** The dreamer himself at that age. If he concentrates on his life at that age, he may recall details that are relevant to the rest of the dream.

Someone looking younger in the dream than in life: ** Back to the time when he or she was that age.

Although the whole of a person's life is spread out for the dream mind to dip into where it likes, younger people's dreams are actually inclined to look ahead more, while those of older people look back.

The Past Dreams are not interested in the past as such, so reference to the past will always indicate that the incident is still relevant and either may be used to throw light on the present situation or, more important, may indicate that the past incident is still playing an intense part in the dreamer's present emotional life.

TOOLS (plough, hammer, etc.) ** The male organ: 'tool'.

TOYS ** Childhood; therefore perhaps something in the dreamer that has remained arrested, childlike.

Animals: ** Instincts and desires that are still in an embryonic state; the make-believe and fantasy of childhood that should have been a preparation for mature emotional development have stultified here. This is often true of intuitive intellectuals.
Doll: What the dreamer does to a doll may refer to what he did, or wanted to do, to someone in childhood, perhaps a parent.
Gun: ** The individual's attitude to masculine sexuality is that it's just a toy.

TRANSFORMATION (Metamorphosis) One thing turning into another: *** The two things are linked: both express the same idea in different ways; the different aspects or features of an archetype, an idea, a person or a situation may be built up in this way. Or the idea expressed in one image will lead to the other. And the metamorphosis is simply a pictorial way of expressing cause and effect. ** Inner development, as with statues (§) coming alive.
For example, something dirty that becomes clean when the dreamer touches it: ** The thing, or whatever it signifies, is no longer a source of moral danger to the individual.
Something beautiful and attractive turning into something odious and repulsive or vice versa: ** The conflict between desire and inhibition. The object will often have a sexual significance.
Men transformed into animals and vice versa: ** The conflict between the animal and human sides of the dreamer's nature. His mind may demand fidelity or chastity while his body would like to gratify his impulses without too much responsibility.
In many fairy tales the prince appears first in the guise of an animal or beast and resumes his real shape only at the end, when the heroine has overcome her resistance and disgust and is able to love the beautiful person inside the hideous body, thus breaking the spell.
The dreamer himself as an animal: ** He considers himself guilty of depraved or 'beastly' behaviour.

Men transformed into women: * Depreciation, belittling the man.

TREASURE ** Whatever is valuable, priceless, often life itself; especially spiritual qualities, such as the capacity to love, the ability to create.

Finding the treasure: May be a reconciling symbol of great value, as for example when the introvert discovers the outside world, or vice versa, possibly saving himself from sterility and regression.

If the treasure seems to have been stolen: ** The dreamer doesn't feel he deserves this inflow of grace, for some quite different reason.

If his attitude to the treasure is commercial; if he thinks of its price or market value: This may rob it of its inner value, as well as revealing the mental block that is making any further progress impossible.

The treasure is usually hard to attain: Because it lies deep in the unconscious and may be the central core of the personality, the Self (§ ARCHETYPES).

TREE ** The 'tree of life', with its widely ramifying branches; the process of growth, development, which is linked with the idea of the family tree that unites the human race.

Especially a pine tree or any tree whose shape is particularly phallic: Masculine sexuality and the male principle. *An oak:* ** The male spirit. Strength, perhaps in a particular man.

If the tree is felled or uprooted: ** Impotence or castration; hence the conflict between the dreamer's masculine and feminine aspects (§ CASTRATION).

A tree: * Wood, the unconscious. The Mother (§ ARCHE-TYPES).

Being rooted: * A loss of liberty; on the other hand, the individual's life, like a tree, cannot bear fruit if it is continually transplanted.

The bark: * The individual's protection against the outside world (persona?).

TUNNEL (Drainpipe, etc.) ** A way through via the unconscious (§ BRIDGE). *Crawling into or out of tunnels, especially if there is water in them :* ** The experience of being born (§ BIRTH); therefore may point to a regressive desire to withdraw from the outside world, back into the security of comfort of some womblike situation. The desire to emerge afresh and make new contact with the outside world.

If the tunnel signifies the vagina, crawling into it : ** Coitus.

UNDERGROWTH ✱✱ Pubic hair, therefore the genitals.

VAMPIRES (Succubi, etc.) ** The Anima, but in her negative and destructive aspect, possibly because she is not receiving sufficient attention (§ ARCHETYPES). * Some underlying incestuous theme (§ NIGHTMARE).

VANISHING ** Thoughts, which also 'vanish' into thin air. The conscious mind may be failing to grasp clearly whatever it is that vanishes.
Someone disappearing or suddenly not there: ** Someone who died and suddenly wasn't there to turn to.

VEGETABLES ** A low form of life.
A 'cabbage': ** A dull woman.

WAR (especially civil war) ** Inner conflict.

WATER *** The uterine fluid, therefore the womb from which life emerges at birth. The primeval waters over which the spirit breathed: that is, matter in its most embryonic form, the silent sway of nature; therefore the dreamer's potential: the unformed, 'fluid' side of his nature from which new life may emerge ('the water of life'). In dreams as in baptism, water is an image of spiritual rebirth as well as of cleansing.

It is also a symbol of the mysterious realm of the feminine – the unconscious and womanhood. * The Mother (§ ARCHE-TYPES).

Especially deep, turbid waters: ** The unconscious, which may be a source of energy. Also, being 'out of one's depth'.

Not enough water: ** Not enough energy, life force. Especially in hot climates water is a symbol of life and growth. From water came life, and water also sustains life.

Emerging on to the land: * Being born (§ BIRTH).

Going down into the water, returning to the water: *** The desire to renew one's strength from the origin and source of all created life, for spiritual rebirth. ** A regressive desire to return to the laxity of the womb. But the two are linked, and the regressive womb fantasy can be conspicuously elevated into its counterpart in the spiritual sphere.

Immersion in water: ** Pregnancy and birth (§). ** Death: being swallowed up, returning whence we came. The mortal danger in exploring the origins of our being; this also involves the promise of rebirth.

Flowing water: ** The comforting and peaceful aspect of

life's movement: quiet, steady, slow (Contrast FLOODS). Urinary fantasies and experience.

A puddle growing to an ocean: ** The increasing pressure of urine (§ JOURNEYS, Boats).

Bathing ** Moral purification.

Canals ** Being born (§ BIRTH).

Dams (etc.) ** Conscious attempts to control the force of the water.

Diving ** Absolution. ** 'Diving down' into the mind, possibly in search of childhood memories.
Diving, completely clothed: * Coitus with a condom.

Drowning * Losing consciousness; pushing everything into the unconscious, forgetting it, repressing it.
Being unable to get back to the surface: * Fear of lunacy.

Floods *** The destructive, negative aspect of the life force. Chaos, boundless catastrophe, usually beyond the dreamer's control, which 'inundates' and 'engulfs' him. The source of the danger may lie in the unconscious and may be involved with regressive or introverted tendencies; or being overwhelmed by other unconscious or instinctive impulses. * Being overwhelmed – 'flooded' – with love. ** The sudden inner necessity for change. Dreams of floods are common around the middle of life, or the change of life, when rigid preconceived ideas must be swept away. If the individual clings on to his old ways and tries to stand his ground at such a time, he will probably drown.

Fountain (or font) ** The Mother (§ ARCHETYPES). Womanhood, or a particular woman. * Rebirth. The inner 'fount' of life, the 'fountain' of youth.

Lake Is the goal of many dreams, a special haven towards which the dreamer is struggling.
In a forest: ** A place of initiation and mystery where the

individual may receive new insights or be completely transformed.

In a valley: * The unconscious has been relegated to an inferior position, below the conscious mind.

Pool * That which mirrors its opposite. Often the unconscious.

Reflections in water

In a series of dreams about looking into water: The dreamer may first see his own face, but often not a very flattering version of it: he may be confronted by the worst side of himself, his particular Shadow (§ ARCHETYPES), who often accompanies dreams about water. Later he may encounter objective nature within himself, the water then being an image of the inner realm that reflects the outside world so perfectly that the reflection is identical with the reality. His Anima, possibly in the form of a mermaid, may be among the fish and other living creatures that loom up to lure him away from the shores of consciousness and intellect, out into the depths of the soul, the unconscious and emotional realms.

If only the reflection is seen: ** An idea that hasn't been realized, that exists only in potential form.

Someone else looking into water: May be trying to see the deeper recesses of the dreamer's mind, but is fooled because what he actually sees is only his own reflection, which perhaps obscures his judgement.

Rivers ** Life, and the twists and turns of fortune. Especially the dreamer's particular destiny, which may be great or small according to the size of the river.

If the dreamer is on the bank: Life may be passing him by, while he is left standing on the bank, failing either to go with it or to get across it.

There may be something desirable on the far bank, but dark menacing water or a deep gorge may lie between the dreamer and his objective: Plumbing the hazardous unknown depths of the spirit may be a necessary prerequisite to reaching the destination (§ CROSSING).

The natural flow of water is downward; if this is emphasized: ** The tendency to take the lowest place. A spirit at one with nature; the valley spirit, the spirit of nature that has more to do with the unconscious than the conscious way.

Sea (ocean) *** The obscure forces of nature; the moods and the mystical powers of the psyche. The matrix of all creatures, their origin and their goal. The original chaos. The cold, inhuman cosmic unconscious.
The depths of the sea: ** Whatever cannot be grasped or comprehended; especially the depths of the unconscious, but occasionally the depths of evil.
Deep water/shallow water: ** The contrast between what is profound and what is superficial.
Waves: ** 'Waves' of emotion, surges of lust.
The tide rising: ** A love or emotion that is on the increase.
Undrinkable or brackish water: ** Something else that will not sustain the individual.

Springs ** Sources of life; mystic healing. It may be this original source, this inner potential, that has to be reached before the course of the individual's destiny can be changed.
* Motherhood.

Swimming ** A sensual activity, therefore sex; and the struggle with basic impulses, or other complications. He may or may not be 'keeping his head above water'.
Swimming against the stream or with the tide dragging him away from the shore: ** The struggle is against odds.
The shore or bank: Usually the goal where the complications will be resolved, the ideas put into practice.
* Sadomasochism.
*Childhood, and the terrors of first learning to swim.
Floating, drifting with the current: * Being carried (§).

Swimming Pool ** Womb (§).

Wading (exposed to the waves) ** A full bladder.
In a woman's dream: ** The premenstrual state.

Wells ** The resources and gifts that are of great value to the dreamer.

If the well is dried up, the rope is broken, or the bucket leaks:
** He can find no way of making use of his talents. His uprightness, honour, sincerity and other virtues may be going to waste.

Treasure concealed in the depths of the well: ** Some special grace, not much involved with the individual's merit, that may be retrieved from that source, to be used in the service of the powers that be.

* The Mother (§ ARCHETYPES).

WAX ** Being like 'wax' in somebody's hands.
Waxworks: * Death.

WEAPONS ** Aggression, sometimes amounting to the desire to kill someone; a death wish. *** Masculine sexuality, with all its associations of manliness: being constant, upright, brave, as well as aggressive; but may also evoke for the individual other underlying meanings of the nature of sexuality that the conscious mind so far has failed to grasp.

The background: Should help make it clear whether the image has sexual implications – for example, if the weapons are suddenly flourished in the bedroom.

The emotion that accompanies the dream: Should help pinpoint the meaning of the image.

Rusty weapons, a lack of ammunition, etc.: ** A feeling of sexual inferiority.

Any instrument, such as a spade or pitchfork, used as a weapon: ** The conflict between the productive and creative side of the dreamer and the aggressive and destructive aspects of his personality and psyche.

A sword, an arrow or a club: ** The weapons that a youthful consciousness may use in its fight against the dark unconscious principle (Jung).

Arrow ** Love: one of Cupid's arrows. The male libido.
Being wounded by an arrow: * A harmful state of introversion.

Gun (cannon, etc.) *** The phallus, which it resembles in

shape and in the way it functions. This common image emphasizes the link between aggression and sexuality.

Cartridges that are too large for the gun: * A disproportion between the male and the female genital organs.

Knives

If they are 'bright', 'sharp', 'piercing': ** These same qualities of mind.

Two knives: ** Two death wishes, possibly one directed at whoever is making the dreamer's life unbearable and the other directed against the dreamer himself, a suicidal impulse.

Sword *** Erection, which also penetrates the flesh. * Power or justice: the 'sword' of justice.

WEDDINGS (Marriage) *If something prevents the wedding, usually in a woman's dream:* ** She can't conceive of herself as married; the idea fills her with apprehension (§ OBSTACLES). * A spiritual union or conjunction, especially where there is mention of offspring from the union. * Ideas about death. In dreams weddings and funerals may stand for each other as equally ceremonious occasions.

WEIGHING (Weight) ** The scales of justice; the conscience.

'Weight': * Importance. 'Weighty' matters may appear in a dream as heavy objects.

WHEEL ** The dynamic principle of movement. The wheel of fortune. The Self, the integrated inner being (§ SHAPES, Circle).

WIND

A gentle breeze: ** The breath of life, the spirit.

Wind over water: ** The living spirit that penetrates inert matter and makes it fertile. This may signify new life stirring in the depths of the dreamer's inner mind that may bring healing changes with it.

Wind: ** Change, transformation: 'the wind of change'.

Strong winds, tempests: ** Anger and upheaval. Possibly an era of destruction that may prepare the way for new beginnings.

The four winds: § NUMBERS, Four.

A Tight WIRE Tension and insecurity.

WITCH ** Mother. Every child experiences an overwhelming magical power in regard to its mother. She may be seen as a good or evil witch, depending not so much on her actual qualities as on the way the individual is experiencing her then.

* The Terrible Mother (§ ARCHETYPES).

In a woman's dream: * The embodiment of repressed sexual desire, especially towards her father.

WOMB If the dreams and fantasies about returning to the womb can only be exalted to the archetypal level, dedicated to the Great Mother, Mother Earth herself, or some personal equivalent; if the inertia can be associated with the passive principle of nature, the yielding but also the receptive; if the womb itself can be seen in its symbolic perspective as the primeval swamps from which man evolved in a long slow process, then the period of relaxation and rest can become meaningful. In the arms of Nature herself the infantile no longer seems so petty. And relying on Nature's many ways of self-healing, the period of regression need not foreshadow total atrophy of the conscious mind, but may become just a time for lying fallow and mustering one's resources from that great source of energy, the unconscious soul.

WOOD All wooden objects may have the same symbolic significance as the tree (§).

WOODS (Forests)

The dark wood that turns into a primeval forest: ** Entry into the unconscious (§ PLACE, Jungles).

WORDS

Words, phrases, sentences, etc., used in dreams have often actually been said in the dreamer's waking life. The figure who says them in the dream may in fact be a substitute for the person who said them in real life.

Whether or not the sentences are assembled from phrases the individual has actually heard, whatever is said in a dream is often the voice of conscience.

Thus, admonitions, warnings, threats: ** The dreamer's conscience.

Words that can't be heard clearly enough to be understood: ** Something the dreamer has failed to understand or may be refusing to understand.

Advice

To the dreamer: As this is also supplied by the dreamer and only put into the mouth of the other person (§ ACTION), it may be a hypocritical way of trying to put the responsibility on to someone else, especially where the advice is to be self-indulgent, for example.

If the dreamer gives advice: It may reveal his real attitude.

Condensed (or newly coined) Words

Dreams often elide words but always significantly, so the individual should note the mutilated words accurately as they are, before looking for resemblances to other words or associations.

Forbidden Words

*** A strong desire to do whatever is forbidden. Even more in dreams than in life, what is forbidden is a way of exciting interest and provoking disobedience, it's a way of calling particular attention to something (§ NEGATIVES).

Opinions

Are not usually distorted at all by dreams and so may reveal what the rest of the dream is about.

Quarrel ** Inner conflict: contradictory impulses within the dreamer. He may be trying to throw off some part of his upbringing or conditioning.

†: Personal values v. principles instilled from outside.

A wife quarrelling with a girlfriend or ex-girlfriend: Loyalty to wife v. passion for girlfriend.

Making a Report * The dreamer wishes to make a clean breast of something.

Reproaches ** Self-reproaches, guilt.

Thus, a woman accusing a male dreamer of being cold: ** Shame about his passion being actually on the wane.

Voice *An authoritative voice, although the dreamer cannot see who is speaking:* The Wise Old Man (§ ARCHETYPES). There may be something final and indisputable about the character of what is said. *A quiet voice:* ** The 'still, small voice of conscience'.

Wordplay If any word that the dreamer finds himself using to describe his dream also has another meaning, this other meaning may make more sense in the dream. The interchange of words is not necessarily absolutely accurate: the dream takes no notice of different spellings, omitted or added letters. For instance, 'bamboos' swaying in the wind: * 'bamboozle'.

WOUNDS (bleeding, limps, scars, blindness, etc.)

In a man's dream: ** Castration. Mutilation, scars, being blinded, are not differentiated in dreams from castration (§).

In the case of Jews: * Circumcision; the dream may refer to their heritage.

A limp or lame animal: ** Fear of impotence or emasculation, being degraded, humiliated; *mutilation of an animal, however, such as cutting off a lion's paw:* * Mortification of the flesh.

Bleeding, in women's dreams especially: ** Defloration, loss of virginity. Menstruation, therefore the feminine realm.

Being wounded: ** Being 'wounded' by love, especially if an arrow is involved. Or other psychological wounds: 'wounded' vanity. Wounds inflicted by ourselves. Or, rarely: * The wounds of Christ, and his redeeming blood.

If the wounds heal: ** The forces at work on behalf of the dreamer are adequate.

Scars: ** Lasting mental effects.

Occasionally before surgery people have dreamed about being wounded.

WRONG *Going into the wrong class, catching the wrong bus, etc.:* ** Misconduct; doing something morally wrong.

Bibliography

Sigmund Freud, *The Interpretation of Dreams*, James J. Strachey, trans. (New York: Avon, 1967). The pioneer work.

Carl G. Jung, *Collected Works*, published in several volumes (New York: Pantheon, Bollingen Series). Jung stated that he did not have the time to arrange his material systematically and that this would be the responsibility of those who came after him. The present dictionary has collected and arranged some of his many insights into the meaning of dreams.

In addition to the works of Freud and Jung, the following are some important contributions to the field of dream analysis:

Gerhard Adler, *Studies in Analytical Psychology* (New York: Putnam, 1967).

Leon L. Altman, *The Dream in Psychoanalysis* (New York: International Universities Press, 1969).

Artemidorus, *The Interpretation of Dreams* (London: Bernard Alsop). (§ ANIMALS, Sheep.)

Raymond De Becker, *The Understanding of Dreams*, Michael Heron, trans. (New York: Hawthorn, 1968).

Nandor Fodor, *New Approaches to Dream Interpretation* (New York: Citadel Press, 1951). (§ BIRTH.) Also specializes in the complexity of numbers in dreams.

Erich Fromm, *The Forgotten Language* (New York: Holt, Rinehart & Winston, 1951). Light and introductory. The author believes that dream language should be taught in schools like any other foreign language, but this would require a dictionary, however ambiguous or incomplete.

Georg Groddeck, *The Book of the It* (New York: NAL Mentor, 1962). Not much about dreams, but fascinating on the powers of the unconscious mind – enough to convince anyone that it is worth tuning in to what it is saying in dreams. (§ ILLNESS.)

Emil Gutheil, *The Handbook of Dream Analysis* (New York: Liveright, 1970). Many good examples of dream interpretation in action.

Calvin S. Hall, *The Meaning of Dreams* (New York: McGraw-Hill, 1966). The clearest discussion of the pictorial language and principles of interpretation.

Jolande Jacobi, *The Way of Individuation*, R. F. Hull, trans. (New York: Harcourt, Brace & World, 1967). A clear account of the process of becoming whole, by discovering, partly through dreams, and then fulfilling one's potential.

Ernest Jones, *On the Nightmare* (New York: Liveright, 1951).

Susanne K. Langer, *Philosophy in a New Key: A Study of the Symbolism of Reason, Rite and Art* (Cambridge, Mass.: Harvard University Press, third edition, 1957). A reappraisal of all that is beyond the range of the rational intellect as it is usually applied to philosophy.

John Layard, *The Lady of the Hare* (London: Faber & Faber, 1944). An excellent story of a curious and fascinating series of dreams. (§ FAMILY.)

Irles Pedro Mesuguer, S.J., *The Secret of Dreams* (London: Burns & Oates, 1960). Offers reassurance to Catholics doubtful about dabbling in dream analysis.

Wilhelm Stekel, *The Interpretation of Dreams*, Eden and Cedar Paul, trans. (New York: Washington Square Press); also available in two volumes titled *The Interpretation of Dreams: New Developments and Technique* (New York: Liveright, 1943). The first to use a more intuitive approach, the author thus covers more ground but cannot fully substantiate his hypotheses.

Edward C. Whitmont, *The Symbolic Quest* (New York: Putnam, 1969). This clarifies and substantiates the concept of the Archetypes.

One valuable book which has appeared since the original publication of this dictionary:

Patricia Garfield, *Creative Dreaming* (London: Futura, 1976). More useful research about how to recall dreams, and investigates ways of controlling your dream life. This book forms a natural bridge to the use of 'active imagination' and understanding the wider significance of symbolism in everyday life. See my *Dictionary of Symbols*.

Index